GLIMPSES OF ETERNITY

STUDIES IN THE PARABLES OF JESUS

PAUL EARNHART

Glimpses of Eternity: Studies in the Parables of Jesus
© 2012 by DeWard Publishing Company, Ltd.
P.O. Box 6259, Chillicothe, Ohio 45601
800.300.9778
www.deward.com

Cover design by Jonathan Hardin.

All rights reserved. No portion of this book may be reproduced in any form without written permission from the publisher.

Reasonable care has been taken to trace original sources for any excerpts and quotations appearing in this book and to document such information. For material not in the public domain, fair-use standards and practices were followed. Should any attribution be found to be incorrect or incomplete, the publisher welcomes written documentation supporting correction for subsequent printings.

Printed in the United States of America.

ISBN: 978-1-936341-41-2

The Parables of Jesus:
Glimpses of Eternity

Jesus was not a soldier or a statesman or a merchant. He was a teacher, unique and incomparable, but a teacher (Matt 4.23). Those who heard Him were "astonished at his teaching; because he taught them as one having authority, and not as their scribes" (Matt 7.29). Even His enemies reported that they had never heard a man speak as He did (John 7.46). And why not? He was heaven's message incarnate—the Word become flesh (John 1.14). In Jesus men saw, as well as heard, the truth. Word and thought and deed were marvelously one in Him. And in His voice were the confident echoes of eternity. He both knew, and was, the Truth (John 14.6).

As a teacher, the mission of the Son of God was to reveal His father's heart to men, to cause them to know and understand His gracious will for their lives. Such understanding could not be created by divine fiat. The wonders Jesus worked were remarkable, but they served only to confirm His message (John 3.1–2) which, as the true source of God's saving energy (Rom 1.16), had at last to be accepted and understood to be effective (John 6.44–45). For all their magnificent display of divine power, miracles could not force that understanding. It had to be achieved by patient and often laborious instruction which, even after long hours, days, and months, was subject to complete rejection.

But out of the persevering love of His heart, Jesus sought to make all men understand, and chose approaches which were remarkable for their simplicity. He took men where they were and sought to lead them to where they needed to be. He used their knowledge of this world to teach them about the next. There is nothing in Jesus' style as a teacher that is a greater expression of this than His parables, and those who would understand Jesus must come at last to understand those powerful illustrative stories which became the characteristic vehicle of so many of His lessons. The parables of Jesus have passed into history and become an intrinsic part of our culture. He could have been immortalized in the annals of literature for them alone. But for all their celebrity, they are as little understood by this generation as by that one to which they were first addressed.

"Parable," the anglicized form of the Greek word, *parabole*, derives from a Greek verb which means "to place beside, to cast alongside." A parable is a story which places one thing beside another for the purpose of teaching. It is a comparison, putting the known beside the unknown. Memorably expressed, it is "an earthly story with a heavenly meaning."

The Greek word for parable occurs some fifty times in the New Testament, only twice outside the gospels (Heb 9.9; 11.19, where it is translated "figure," KJV, ASV). In Mark 4.23 it is construed as "proverb" (KJV, NIV). It is characteristically understood of "a somewhat lengthy… narrative drawn from nature or human circumstances, the object of which is to set forth a spiritual lesson" but it is also "used of a short saying or proverb" (W. E. Vine, *Expository Dictionary of NT Words*, p. 158).

Because of the uncertainty of what exactly constitutes a parable, the lists that have been compiled of Jesus' parables vary in length with the judgment of the compiler. The longer lists include such illustrations as "the good shepherd" (John 10) and the "two builders" (Matt 7.24–27). The shorter lists exclude them. Trench, in his now classic work, *Notes on the Parables of Jesus*, lists only thirty.

If we cannot determine with exact certitude whether some illustrations of Jesus deserve to be called parables, there are some things about parables that are beyond doubt.

Parables are not fables or myths. There are no unreal elements or impossible situations in them. In fact, their strength lies in the absolute conceivability and likelihood of the circumstances which they describe. They speak of familiar, real life situations.

Parables are more than proverbs, though at times similar in design. In the gospels, proverbs are sometimes referred to as "parables"—"Physician, heal yourself" (Luke 4.23); "If the blind lead the blind, both shall fall into the ditch" (Matt 15.14–15); "No man tears a patch from a new garment and sews it on an old one"; "And no one pours new wine into old wineskins…" (Luke 5.36–37). But a proverb is characteristically a short, pithy saying whose meaning is evident. A parable tends to be longer, more involved, and the meaning not so easily seen.

Jesus, so far as we know, did not begin to teach in parables until near the end of the second year of His public ministry (there is a lone exception, Luke 7.41–42). It was in the presence of an immense multitude near the Sea of Galilee, and His illustrative comparisons came with a rush that startled His disciples (Matt 13). In marvelously concrete and simple stories, Jesus unfolded for His followers the mysteries of the kingdom of heaven. It was to be only the beginning. This is an invitation to study those wonderful narratives which invite us to look into the very heart of God.

Why Parables?

When Jesus, toward the end of His second year of public preaching, poured out beside the Sea of Galilee that marvelous series of parables illustrating the nature of the kingdom of heaven, His disciples were so taken aback by them that they asked him privately, "Why do you speak to them in parables?" (Matt 13.10; Mark 4.10).

Parables certainly had a special place in the latter phase of Jesus' teaching, but they were not unique to Him. They appear frequently in the Old Testament (see 2 Samuel 12.1–4), especially in the prophets (Isa 5.1–2; Ezek 17.1–10), and were a familiar method of teaching among the rabbis of Jesus' own time. What, then, must have surprised the disciples was not their unfamiliarity with parables, but the sudden shift to an approach heretofore uncharacteristic of their Teacher. Jesus attributes the change in teaching to a change in the attitude of His hearers.

Matthew says that Jesus spoke in parables as a fulfillment of prophecy: "I will open my mouth in parables; I will utter things hidden from the foundation of the world" (Matt 13.34–35; Psa 78.2). The purpose of the parables was to reveal the hidden truths of God's kingdom, but not to everyone. To the honest heart these illustrative stories would bring further light, but to the proud and rebellious they would increase confusion (Matt 13.11–17). That is the meaning of Jesus' statement that "to you it is given to know the mysteries of the kingdom of heaven, but to them it is not given" (13.11). This has no reference to some kind of arbitrary Calvinistic predestination but to a principle which fills the pages of the Old Testament. Isaiah speaks powerfully of it. "For thus saith the high and lofty One that inhabiteth eternity, whose name is Holy: I dwell in the high and holy place, with him also that is of a contrite and humble spirit, to revive the spirit of the humble, and to revive the heart of the contrite" (57.15). "But to this man I will look, even to him that is poor and of a contrite spirit, and that trembles at my word" (66.2). And as for the proud, Isaiah says that in the coming Messianic kingdom "the lofty looks of man shall be brought low, and the haughtiness of men shall be bowed down..." (2.11).

The passage in Isaiah which Jesus quotes to explain His sudden reversion to parables (6.9–10) speaks of the spiritual degradation of Israel, of the pride and stubbornness of heart which made it impossible for them any longer to hear and understand the words of God. Jesus says plainly that it was a prophecy which had been liberally fulfilled in His own hearers. All the wisdom they heard from His mouth and all the marvels they saw from His hand had meant nothing because their heart was "waxed gross, and their ears are dull of hearing, and their eyes they have closed" (Matt 13.15).

The parables were a fan in the hand of the Son of God, a fan that would cleanse His threshing floor of the chaff while it purified the grain. They were a probing two-edged sword to determine if the hearts of His hearers were proud or humble, stubborn or contrite (Heb 4.12). That is the meaning of His "whosoever hath, to him it shall be given, and he shall have in abundance: but whosoever hath not, from him shall be taken away even that which he hath" (Matt 13.12). Those who possessed a lowliness of mind were destined to have a rich and true understanding of the kingdom of heaven, but those who had none or little of that spirit were destined to lose even the little understanding that they had.

The gospel of the kingdom is so fashioned as to attract and inform the humble while it drives off and confuses the proud. Hearing the word of God is a dynamic experience. We will be either the better or the worse for it. The same sun that melts the wax hardens the clay. But that is the choice the student, not the teacher, makes. The parables will not make a humble heart proud, but they can make a proud heart humble if we are disposed to let them. That, of course, is the ultimate wish of the Savior of men.

The meaning of the parables was not always patently evident, even to the humble heart, but the same story that sent the haughty away laughing smugly brought the humble back asking questions. The disciples of Jesus did not understand why He suddenly began teaching exclusively in parables (Matt 13.10, 34–35), or what His unusual stories meant, but they had that simplicity of heart which brought them back asking for more information (Matt 13.36; Mark 4.10; Luke 8.9). We have that choice, too. When we are confronted with some challenging statement of Scripture, we can either leave in despair and confusion, or stay around patiently to learn more. Our response will reveal whether it is given to us to know the mysteries of the kingdom of God, and what kind of heart we have.

Lessons That Turned the Lights Out

It must be plainly said that the parables were designed to put some people's lights out. These stories baffled and annoyed those dishonest souls who were eager to abuse whatever little truth seemed to filter down to them (Matt 13.10–15; Mark 4.11–12; Luke 8.10). And we mustn't think of them as religious illiterates who were morally depraved. In their number were the most religious and apparently pious people of the times. But they had an agenda that differed from God's.

After the Lord taught His great parable of the *Shepherd and the Sheep-Fold*, a discourse which seems to have come in the winter before the spring of His death (John 10.1–18), His critics complained that His teaching was obscure and confusing and that He should tell them in plain language whether He was the Christ or not. Jesus' reply was to the point: I have told you in a hundred ways, He said, but none of them will suffice because you simply do not believe; and you do not believe because you are not of my sheep (10.24–26). The Son of God was not interested in forcing down the throats of unbelieving men what they positively did not want. This great Shepherd was calling only to those who would hear His voice and follow Him (10.27). To the rest, His words would simply be so much gobbledy-gook; not because it was, but because their carnal ears had no spiritual frequencies.

The same point is aptly made by another incident that occurred during that same winter—the Lord's healing of the blind beggar in Jerusalem at the pool of Bethesda (John 9). Jesus' critics sought feverishly at first to discredit this remarkable healing (the man had been blind from birth) as a ruse, but, totally stymied by the testimony of the man's own parents, they were reduced to arguing mindlessly that what everybody in town knew had happened, had not really happened because it was done on the wrong day

(Sabbath) by the wrong man (Jesus). Out of nothing but blind, unyielding stubbornness they denied the undeniable. Jesus was later to say to them: "For judgment came I into this world, that they that see not may see; and that they that see may become blind" (9.38). His Jewish critics, not quite so dull that absolutely nothing penetrated, finally caught the drift. "Are we also blind?" they asked. To which the Lord replied, "If you were blind, you would have no sin; but now you say, 'We see.' Therefore your sin remains" (9.40–41).

As we have already noted, Jesus' parables never appealed much to people who knew it already. They simply served to put out the little light that such folk had, but that was alright because the Lord was not calling them anyway, and the time had come by the third year of His public ministry to drive off the eternal critics, the curiosity seekers, the unthinking hangers-on who had no real interest in the kingdom of God. The hour had arrived when the true disciples had to be gathered around Him and prepared for the unthinkable horror to come.

Accordingly, Edersheim *(Life and Times of Jesus the Messiah,* Vol. II, p. 579–580) classifies the parables of Jesus along a continuum of the increasing hostility of His opponents:

1. The seven parables of Matthew 13 on the nature of the kingdom of God (late second year) were spoken just after the Pharisees had resorted to explaining away Jesus' miracles as demonic (Matt 12.22–34).

2. The parables spoken after the transfiguration (third year) are found in Luke, chapters 10–16 and 18. These are about the kingdom, but have an admonitory thrust and controversial tone in response to the growing enmity of the Pharisees.

3. There are eight parables (Matthew 18.20–22, 24–25 and Luke 19) in which the controversial element dominates and the evangelistic aspect recedes. They take on the theme of judgment.

A.B. Bruce *(The Parabolic Teachings of Christ)* sees them as also naturally divided into three groups, but according to Jesus' work as a Teacher, an Evangelist, and a Prophet.

The *teaching parables* have to do with the Lord's work in training the Twelve: parables on the kingdom (Luke 11.5–8 and

18.1–8); and three parables which relate to labor and reward in the kingdom—Laborers in the vineyard (Matt 20.1–16), Talents (Matt 24.14), Pounds (Luke 19.12).

The *evangelistic parables* include those that show God's love for sinners: The two debtors (Luke 7.40); lost sheep, lost coin, lost son (Luke 15); the Pharisee and the publican (Luke 18.9–14); The Great Supper (Luke 14.16); the Good Samaritan (Luke 10.30); the Unrighteous Steward (Luke 16.1); and the Unmerciful Servant (Matt 18.23).

The *prophetic parables* contain messages of divine judgment and include: Barren Fig Tree (Luke 13.6); Wicked Husbandman (Matt 21.33); Marriage of the King's Son (22.1); Ten Virgins (25.1); and the Rich Fool (Luke 12.16).

Though Bruce's analysis is not exact, it gives us some helpful suggestions about how to understand the dynamics of Jesus' parables as they relate to what He was attempting to do during the closing months of His work when so many forces were coming into final focus.

Finding Our Way through the Parables

There are some important principles which must guide us if we are to unlock the treasures of the parables. The failure to know and observe the natural guidelines which govern the interpretation of the special kind of literature to which the stories of Jesus belong will produce confusion rather than enlightenment.

A classic example of how not to do it is seen in Augustine's treatment of the parable of the *Good Samaritan*. Ignoring every contextual clue, the great North African allegorized Jesus' simple story into a history of mankind. The man felled by thieves (Satan and his angels) was Adam who had, in rebellion, left Jerusalem (the heavenly city) and headed for Jericho (mortality). Satan had stripped him (of his immortality) and left him half-dead (spiritually, but not physically). The priest and Levite (Old Testament priesthood and ministry) who passed by were incapable of saving the man and it was left to the Samaritan (the Lord) to bind his wounds (restrain from sin), pour on oil (hope) and wine (fervency). The inn is the church, the innkeeper the apostle Paul, and the two pence are either the two greatest commandments or the two "sacraments." No comment on such evident over-reaching is necessary.

The parables of Jesus should be approached naturally, taking care not to derail them from their simple purpose. They are illustrative stories generally conceived to have three basic parts: (1) a historical occasion that produced the parable; (2) the story or narrative; and (3) the principal lesson to be derived from that story. With this in mind, let's look at some important rules to follow in searching out the individual messages of the parables.

1. Study the parable in its historical context to determine why it was spoken. All the parables were first spoken for a particular audience on a particular occasion. For example, the story of the

Good Samaritan was occasioned by a certain lawyer's complaint to Jesus that it was hard to love your neighbor when you couldn't figure out who he was (Luke 10.25–30), and the three wonderful parables about lost things in Luke 15 were a response to the attacks made on Jesus for the disreputable company He was keeping (vv 1–2). Sometimes this background information is wanting and the meaning of a particular parable must be sought from the broader information of the Gospels, but when present, the circumstances in which a parable was spoken give us the very finest clue as to the Lord's purpose for His story. Context must always rule the text.

2. Look for the principal truth that the parable is intended to teach. Most parables are intended to make only one point, not to be the vehicle for the whole scheme of redemption. Secondary lessons can often be legitimately derived from a parable, but this should be done with care and only after the principal message has been determined.

3. Don't try to make the parable "walk on all fours." The details of a parable may at times have significance, but as often as not they contain no hidden meaning and are simply intended to fill out the story. The fatted calf, music and dancing, gold ring, and shoes and robe of the story of the Prodigal Son are not symbolic of anything, but simply reflect, in terms meaningful for the times, the joy of the father at his son's return. A good rule is not to give some special figurative meaning to a detail unless the context warrants it.

4. Don't try to establish a doctrinal position solely by a parable. There is much that is made clearer to us by the parables of Jesus, but they must always be understood in the light of the clear teachings of Scripture, never in contradiction to them. These illustrations are more intended to be windows than foundation stones. They do not so much declare a doctrine as they illustrate a significant facet of it.

5. Finally, and most importantly, always make a personal application of each parable. After having determined the correct lesson or lessons of the parable under study, the most important

question is: "Have I met myself in this parable?" "What changes in my life and thinking does this parable demand of me?" There is nothing as tragic as a study of the teachings of Jesus which is driven by nothing more than intellectual curiosity unless it is the study of some preacher who feels the "professional" need to preach a sermon to others without a single thought of making any application to himself. It is imperative in our study of the parables that we each continually ask, "Lord, what is there here for me?" In this way alone will we find the hearing ears for which our Lord appealed when first He taught in parables (Mark 4.9, 23).

Jesus Had a Word for It

Jesus likely lived more mindfully of the world in which He walked than any other man before or since. And out of His profound awareness of all that surrounded Him He drew the rich metaphors that made Him such a compelling illustrator and teacher.

The Lord began early in His public discourses to speak knowingly of fishermen and farmers and shepherds and merchants. He drew expressive comparisons from the world of kings and princes, servants and paupers, priests and publicans, judges and thieves. He found lessons in grass and flowers, in birds and trees, in wind and rock. He spoke much of vineyards and grain fields, and of tares and thorns and thistles. He knew well the place of the fox and the way of wolves and sheep. And especially He spoke of home—of salt and lamps and cooking and cleaning, of feasts and weddings, and fathers and children. And His words were wonderful in the way they made the will of Heaven so real and clear.

Much that Jesus said so expressively was not in classic parables, but in sayings and illustrations that were similar to them. A.B. Bruce calls them "parable-germs" and G. Campbell Morgan styles them "parabolic illustrations." Many are simply passing metaphors that add clarity to a thought, a teaching. The first appears in the Lord's call to four Galileans to become "fishers of men" (Matt 4.19). The Sermon on the Mount is absolutely full of these rich analogies, comparisons that make the thought virtually jump from the page. It is to these seminal "parables" of Jesus that we first want to give our attention.

The Friends of the Bridegroom (Matt 9.15)
Suddenly, in the midst of the rising popularity of the Lord's second year of preaching and the success of the great Galilean ministry, the synoptists interrupt their story to tell us that all is not

well. In Matthew 9, Mark 2, and Luke 5, each one begins for the first time to tell of the growing opposition to Jesus in the Jewish establishment. He did not fit comfortably into their traditional world. His completely unorthodox background and behavior had made the Jewish leaders very uncomfortable, but His proposal to forgive the sins of a palsied man in Capernaum made the observer team sent down from Jerusalem well nigh apoplectic! This was blasphemy! (Matt 9.1–8; Mark 2.1–12; Luke 5.17–26). They would have said more, but Jesus had completely healed the man before their very eyes!

Matters were not improved later when He selected Matthew, the publican, as one of His close associates and then spent the evening feasting happily with other such disreputable types (Matt 9.27–32).

It was there, perhaps near Matthew's gate, that the Pharisees, in strange league with some of John's disciples, ask Him why they and John's disciples fasted while His own followers were feasting and rejoicing (Matt 9.14; Mark 2.18; Luke 5.33). Jesus answered that it was not appropriate for the bridegroom's friends to mourn at the wedding feast while the bridegroom was with them. There would be time enough to fast and be sad, He said, when their friend was taken from them.

The Pharisees and the disciples of John had tried to judge Jesus by their own standards. Who gave Him the right to break the proprieties? What kind of holy man is this who feasts His days away? One might understand the disciples of the Baptist. With John languishing in Herod's prison, they doubtless felt fasting more appropriate than feasting and perhaps had been made to wonder at Jesus' apparent unconcern. The Pharisees, on the other hand, were just mindless ritualists who had a twice-a-week habit by which they sought credit with God (Luke 18.9–12; tradition had it that Moses ascended Sinai on Monday and descended on Thursday). It had nothing to do with their hearts or the spiritual realities of their lives. Their fasts, like those of the ancient Israelites (Isa 58.1–9), held no earnest longing toward God.

It made some sense for the disciples of John to fast. Their master's message had been a call to repentance. There was comfort in it, but a sobering comfort. The kingdom of heaven was at hand, but who was prepared to meet it? It was a needed message, but not the whole of what Heaven had to say.

And it was altogether proper for the Pharisees to fast, for the Lord's way was to them a burden grievous to be borne. They certainly knew nothing of what Jesus described as "a well of water springing up unto everlasting life" (John 4.14). But it was not right for the friends of the Bridegroom to be sad. Jesus had come to bring fullness of joy (John 15.11). And it was the joy of the greatest wedding of all—the marriage of earth and heaven! The day would come when there would be no need to tell His disciples to fast—the storm was already gathering that would take the Bridegroom from them. But even that would not be able to take away the deep peace, the exulting joy that He had given them (John 14.27–28; 15.11; 16.21–22). The wedding feast would resume at last in a burst of triumph—beginning with an empty tomb and ending in a blaze of eternal glory (Rev 19.6–9; 21.1–4). Christians, rejoice!

An Invitation to Joy

The question raised by the disciples of John about the feasting ways of Jesus and His disciples in a time that they saw as full of tragedy (Matt 9; Mark 2; Luke 5) was later to issue in a plaintive inquiry from the imprisoned John himself. "Are you the one who is to come, or shall we look for another?" (Matt 11.3). It was the longing cry of one whose sufferings had apparently made him doubt for a moment the very King and kingdom which he had himself heralded. After answering John's question, Jesus spoke of his unique greatness to the gathered crowd and then rebuked them by observing that they were like stubborn children at their games who refused to play either wedding or funeral (Matt 11.16–19). John had come fasting and living apart and they had said that he was possessed by a demon. Jesus had come feasting and living freely among them and they had complained that He was a glutton and companion of sinners!

There is no question but that Jesus identified His mission and message as one of joy. He is the true bridegroom who has invited us to a wedding feast. He came to bring peace to the troubled, forgiveness to the guilty, joy to the downcast, freedom to the enslaved (Isa 61.1–3). The message of John, and the fasting of John and his disciples, had been entirely appropriate at one time—and still is when men and women in their stubbornness and pride need to repent and humble themselves before a holy and righteous God. But it does not make sense for those who have humbled themselves in deep remorse to continue the funeral when "the Lamb of God who takes away the sin of the world" has come (John 1.29).

It is ironic that it was John the Baptist himself who had earlier said, "I am not the Christ. ...He that is the friend of the bridegroom, that stands and hears him, rejoices greatly because of the bridegroom's voice: this my joy is therefore made full. He must increase, but I must decrease" (John 3.28–30). Why were these disciples of this very John still fasting and grieving? Because they had not yet believed that Jesus was the Christ of God. In their doubtful minds the "bridegroom" was not yet with them. Unlike their teacher, they had not yet come to know and rejoice in Him.

There are still people who have trouble getting past John to Jesus. It is certainly true of contemporary members of the "Baptist" party who defend their sectarian name and spirit by appealing beyond the Christ to John the Baptist. It may have been once appropriate to be a disciple of the Baptist, but now that the Son of God Himself has come it is wholly without justification (Acts 19.1–5). John would have been the first to reprove it. Acts 11.26 says "the disciples were called Christians...."

The same is true of all those who revere men who speak of Christ above Christ Himself. There is absolutely no defense for men gladly calling themselves Lutherans or Wesleyans, et. al., or, more subtly, quietly esteeming contemporary preachers and their judgments above the person and will of God. "He that glories, let him glory in the Lord" (1 Cor 1.31; see 1.11–13).

But there is an even more fundamental problem addressed in Jesus' answer to the disciples of John. Jesus said that to be with Him was to have joy. Yet there are Christians who have accepted the invitation to the Lord's wedding feast, but seem unwilling to give up the funeral march. They seem determined to live in perpetual grief and despair for their inadequacies and failures. The Lord's invitation to celebrate and exult in His mercy is certainly not a call to live with a casual indifference to sin, but neither is it a summons to perpetual breast-beating once we have repented and sought His forgiving love.

It is not fitting that Christians should live in the very presence of the Lord as a defeated and despairing people. Such behavior becomes a slander to His loving kindness.

It is also not fitting that the people of God should serve Him like "slaves scourged to their dungeon," performing their service to Him as an onerous, burdensome duty. Such conduct is a defamation of His grace, a dishonoring libel of His love. To truly live in the happy fellowship of the Son of God is to know that His "yoke is easy" and His "burden is light" (Matt 11.30).

It may indeed not be possible to command an emotion, but it is possible to command that we look earnestly at the great truths about God that will, in so doing, bring us inevitable joy. So Paul says to the Philippians, "Rejoice in the Lord always; again I say, Rejoice" (4.4). It is simply not right for Christians to be perpetually sad and disconsolate, whatever may be their burdens. Paul is right to say that there is enough joy in Christ to completely overwhelm all our heartaches. As our Lord Himself said, there are some things that are just not appropriate when you are living in loving fellowship with the King of the universe.

New Wine and Old Wineskins

When Jesus said that He came "to cast fire upon the earth" (Luke 12.49), and "not to send peace but a sword" (Matt 10.34), how truly He spoke. He did not fit the familiar ways of the world into which He came. Even the most revolutionary thought of His times could not contain Him. His words and ways were transcendently different, disquieting, threatening. There could be no quiet synthesis of the old and the new, only an uncompromising collision which would lead inevitably to either rebellion or surrender. Some would come to love the new, others to hate it.

In His three analogies in Matthew 9.14–17 (Mark 2.18–22; Luke 5.33–39), Jesus answers His critics gently, but illustrates the inevitability of the conflict: How can the bridegroom's friends mourn at the wedding feast? How can new cloth be used to patch an old garment? How can explosive new wine be contained in old inflexible wineskins?

Jesus' proverb about the new patch on an old garment could have easily arisen from His own life. The one who had "no place to lay His head" would have been no stranger to patched robes. And everyone knew that an attempt to patch a worn garment with new cloth would bring two disasters, one structural, and the other aesthetic. The new cloth would shrink at the first washing and put such strain on the old cloth as to make a worse tear than ever (Mark 2.21); and, by its very newness, the fresh patch would make the old garment appear even more faded and worn (Luke 9.36). There are times when the old is irreparable and must simply give place to the new.

Rabbinic Judaism with its Pharisaic corruptions was beyond recovery. Its whole attitude was so far removed from the spirit of the law and the prophets that the only way to get beyond it was to get out of it. And although John's message of repentance and broken-hearted contrition was from God and vital for its time, it was preparatory, not permanent (Acts 18.25–26; 19.1–5). The new way of Jesus was a whole cloth, not a patchwork quilt. He had not come to graft His new truths on the outworn religious fabric of human traditions and ungodly attitudes or to sit motionless at one of the way stations of God's eternal purpose. To have done so would have destroyed everything. In Christ all things were to be made new (2 Cor 5.17).

The unbelieving Jewish establishment refused to relinquish their traditional ways in order to receive the word of God and they crucified Jesus. The Judaizers of the early church were unwilling to give up the law for the gospel and in their effort to accommodate the gospel to the law managed to tear up and destroy everything (Gal 1.6–9; 5.3–4). The same mindset lives today. Old and ungodly ways, refusing to give up the ghost, will challenge us to accommodate the gospel to them or get out. At such times we need to run, not walk, to the nearest exit.

The third of the three proverbs, which Jesus uses to answer His critics, simply reinforces the message of the first two—certain things do not fit together. Men, He said, do not put still fermenting and expanding new wine into old and brittle wineskins because the wineskins will split and be destroyed and the new wine will run out and be lost (Matt 9.17). The Lord is warning that rigid mindsets will cost men the unique specialness of the gospel. Because it is unpredictably new and unimaginable (1 Cor 2.9) and does not fit comfortably into familiar ruts, we are all too disposed to try and force it through our frozen categories until it comes out looking more like we hoped and expected it would.

There is no better way than this to simply spill the precious new wine of God's eternal kingdom upon the ground.

We need to beware of conservatism so mindless that we think the best way to remain sound in the faith is to keep things the way they are. That is all well and good if the way things are is the way the Lord wants them to be; but if not, we need to batten down the hatches and get ready for a long journey into those new places where the Lord intends us to be. The gospel's new wine is not intended to make us comfortable, but to make us new.

Some have made an unfortunate use of Jesus' statement about new wine and old wineskins. For them, the old wineskins often stand for those ways in which New Testament disciples once did things, and the new wine symbolizes the modern ideas which are more appealing to men and women of the current generation. They need to be reminded that all the ways of early Christians which were not simply a reflection of the conditions of their times (the washing of feet as an act of hospitality, a kiss for a greeting, et. al.) were the product of the radical will of Christ and the unchanging eternal principles of His kingdom. We should all do so well as to follow their example (Acts 2.42). For if we do, we will surely not be sitting still, but will be engaged in the most radically transforming experience in human history. To drink the wine of the kingdom of God is not a step of moderation. To obey the voice of the Son of God is not a conservative act!

Expandable Hearts

The gospel's new wine demands an elastic heart—an abiding willingness to look at things afresh and a readiness to make radical changes in thinking and doing when we hear Jesus in His word calling us to follow Him into new spiritual advances. For this reason the word of Christ is to have a perennial newness about it even to the Christian. It will certainly always be threateningly new to the unbelieving world which has a proud tendency to harden its categories against the will of God. But as the Pharisees have amply demonstrated, it is not the irreligious world alone which resists the gospel's intimidating ferment, for no mind has feared the gospel as deeply as entrenched religious traditionalism.

Faith in the Son of God is dynamic, not static, and fellowship with Him a never-ending adventure; not because *He* is changing, but because our comprehension and application of His eternal will must always be growing and enlarging. Whatever God has already accomplished in our lives, it is only preparation for what He is about to do. We are involved in a momentous transformation whose ultimate goal is the image of Christ Himself (Rom 8.29; Eph 4.13–15). Therefore our hearts must always be expandable, ready to receive a new lesson in holiness and purity. We have only begun to be what God wants us to be.

At times, we are tempted to plead with our Father for no more changes, no more challenges, and no more problems. We just want to sit down and enjoy what we have done for a while without the stretching pains of new crises and difficulties. The problem is that this longing for rest can lead to a spiritual hardening which will make our experience with God only a memory. You can see it in Christians who are completely disengaged from present challenges and opportunities, their only spiritual exercise a continual rehashing of the past.

The immensity of what God has in mind for us is powerfully stated in Paul's prayer for the Ephesians: "that you may be strengthened with power through His Spirit in the inward man; that Christ may dwell in your hearts through faith... that you may be filled unto all the fullness of God" (3.16–19). It is no marvel that after this almost incredible petition the apostle delivers the matter into the hands of "him that is able to do exceeding abundantly above all that we ask or think" (3.20). God alone could achieve such a wonder—that by two things, faith and love, we should be filled to the full with the *glories and power* of the eternal Godhead. How much our Father has loved us!

But if we are to be filled with such fullness we must surely offer to God something more than rigid, unyielding hearts. Yesterday's advances in faith and love are old wineskins. They will not suffice to contain the new insights yet to come. Each new day of life is intended to teach us new lessons that make us feel afresh our Father's love. We must greet each one of them with an open and willing heart. The greatness of Christ cannot be poured into the old skins of staid personalities, fixed presuppositions, hardened prejudices, and predetermined ideas. When confronted by a deeper understanding of the will of Christ, rigid old categories can either resist and turn us into mindless religious ideologues or rupture disastrously to the loss of all faith. It is a frightening prospect.

Once the Lord takes up residence in us, a dynamic process begins by which all things are made new (2 Cor 5.17). Because it is a process which must go on as long as we live, there must always be a green edge to us, a living and growing part. It is not a matter of changing with the times, but of moving closer to the timeless. The goal of the race is unmoving, but the runner must always be stretching forward, pressing on, running earnestly toward it (1 Cor 9.24–27; Phil 3.12–14).

We must by all means avoid seeing this great adventure with Christ as running in place, repeating the same old immature and inadequate efforts with ever-increasing intensity. To do so is to repeat the empty-headed folly of the Pharisees who, instead of opening themselves up to a larger understanding of God, became more zealous for their half formed conceptions (Matt 23.23–24). We are never more in danger of this hardening immobility than when we are converted to the church rather than to Christ. Almost without knowing it we can become loyal to the conceptions our brethren have held about things during a particular period in history rather than holding fast to Christ and His word and whatever demands new understanding of the divine will might put upon us. This was the tragedy of the institutional controversy of the 50s and 60s when many Christians, loyal to the system, wanted to continue doing what they should never have been doing in the first place. The same mentality can also prevent us from beginning to do what we should have been doing all along. To be a true follower of Christ demands a flexible, expandable heart. Christ and His will do not change; but we must—continually.

Like Children in the Marketplace

> Whereunto shall I liken the men of this generation, and to what are they like? They are like unto children that sit in the marketplace, and call one to another; who say, "We piped unto you, and ye did not dance; we wailed, and ye did not weep." (Luke 7.31–32)

The resurrection of the widow's son at Nain was one of Jesus' most remarkable miracles, but the report of it had not been sufficient to still the perplexity and doubt of imprisoned John the Baptist. Was this to be the issue of his powerful call for the nation's repentance before the impending arrival for the kingdom of heaven? Where was the axe "laid at the root of the tree," the fiery judgment upon the wicked, and the exaltation of the righteous? He was like a caged lion that, accustomed to roaming free, was being worn down by his lengthening confinement. The miracles of Jesus, no matter how marvelous, may now have seemed to him pedestrian in view of the great expectations which his momentous heralding of the kingdom had created, even in himself.

Jesus' response is gentle but firm, "You must recognize in what I am doing—showing mercy to the oppressed, preaching the gospel to the meek—the prophetic signs of the kingdom of God (Isa 35.5–6; 61.1ff) and you must not be made to stumble because the way I take is not the way you anticipated" (Luke 7.18–23). The Lord then speaks to the multitudes in defense of John. There was nothing soft or weak in him. He was no clever manipulator of popular sentiment. His preaching, fearless and unwavering, often cut against the grain, and he himself lived in comfortless commitment to his immensely significant calling. As the immediate herald of the Messiah he was "more than a prophet" and his greatness among men unsurpassed, but he was not to see the arrival of the kingdom he had so courageously announced. But what he had done was to determine who among the people were prepared to receive it and who were not, and in the process whipped the cover off the hypocritical pretensions of the Pharisees. Jesus' illustration of the new wine and old wineskins was intended to answer the charge that His disciples were lacking in spiritual seriousness because, unlike the Pharisees and disciples of John, they were given to joyful feasting rather than sober fasting. But as soon as it became apparent, it made little difference to Jesus' critics whether He feasted or fasted. It was His very character and teaching that offended them and no change of lifestyle was about to silence their relentless attacks on everything He did.

The insatiable nature of the opposition of the scribes and Pharisees was no more dramatically revealed than in their response to the preaching of John the Baptist. Here should have been the man of their dreams—abstemious, private, reclusive—but, ironically, it was the worldly and openly religious publicans who swarmed happily to his baptism while the Pharisees with their heralded piety refused John's call for repentance (Luke 7.29–30).

It had all become so predictable and so sad. Jesus said that they reminded him of children in the marketplace who refused every game proposed by their companions. They refused to play wedding and they refused to play funeral. The Lord's description of them is not an allegory where the characters must be identified, but an illustration of the kind of mind that does not want to play the game under any circumstances, yet continues to justify the refusal. It had nothing to do with the way John preached or Jesus lived, it was their message of humble repentance that was unacceptable to the self-righteous Pharisees and they were having none of it no matter how it was packaged. They spoke so confidently of God's righteous judgment, but when John came and preached it and called them to repentance they rejected him. They talked longingly of the Messiah, but when He arrived, instead of rejoicing, they caviled and criticized. The Baptist, for them, was a sour "Johnny one-note" with fever of the brain. All he knew was "repent, repent, repent." And with Jesus it was too much joy and forgiveness—too much easy fraternization with the riffraff (Luke

7.33–34). So they filled up the folly of their fathers who piteously begged God for deliverance from Egypt, but when His deliverance appeared they did not like it. Like petulant children, they cried for God, but when He came they did not want Him.

Are we, too, playing the God game? Do we make much claim to wanting Him in our lives, but carp and complain and criticize when someone speaks to us of His demands? And do we cover our rejection of His will with complaints about how it was said or why it was said or who said it? True men and women of God can learn their Savior's will even from their worst enemies! There are too many Christians who are still playing like children in the marketplace. They are not serious. Reversing Paul's admonition to the Corinthians (1 Cor 14.20), in understanding they are like spoiled children, but in malice, jealousy, and strife they have deep experience. Met with the penetrating message of the gospel, they will not grieve for their sins nor rejoice in the wonderful goodness of God. Instead of justifying God, they justify themselves, and so they reveal as did those peevish, self-willed complainers of old that they are not wisdom's children, but the sad misshapen offspring of consummate stupidity (Luke 7.35).

The Kingdom of Heaven: *How It Grows*

The seven parables which Jesus taught beside the Sea of Galilee toward the end of His second preaching year (Matt 13; Mark 4; Luke 8) constitute the richest collection of parables in the Gospels. Strung like pearls on a common theme, they speak of the unique nature of the kingdom of heaven and the special ways in which it grows.

The setting for the teaching of these compelling lessons was magnificent. On the day He had left His home in Capernaum to sit beside the Sea of Galilee and the inevitable throngs pressed around Him. With a fishing vessel for His pulpit and the blue waters of Galilee as a natural amplifier He spoke to the crowds massed on the beach. In the spirit of the Sermon on the Mount, Jesus seeks to help the people understand the specialness of God's kingdom; but now, for the first time, He does it with parables.

Have you ever wondered what happens to the gospel preaching and teaching that goes on in the world? Every day Christians speak to thousands of people. Why does it have so little effect? Has God's word lost its power in this "modern" age? Is there something wrong with the way we are teaching it? Are we not using the proper methods to enlarge the kingdom?

It was questions remarkably similar to these that troubled the imprisoned John the Baptist when he sent his disciples to the Lord to ask if He really was the Messiah or just another forerunner (Matt 11.1–6). All his urgent preaching in the wilderness, the large expectant multitudes, the announcement of heaven's impending kingdom—what had they come to? He was in Herod's prison house for his trouble, and the one on whom he had rested all his hope was just teaching, teaching, teaching. Where was the kingdom? Where was the power? Where was the glory?

Jesus' answer was to the point. He does not seek to steady John's uncertain faith with promises of wonderful things to come. He was doing, He said, exactly what needed to be done. Just as Isaiah had years ago prophesied of the age to come—the sick would be healed (35.5–6) and the poor would have the gospel preached to them (61.1–2). He then adds gently, but firmly, "Blessed is he, whosoever shall find no occasion of stumbling in me" (Matt 11.6).

What the Lord was saying to John's disciples and all others who were listening is that the kingdom of heaven is wholly unlike the kingdoms of this world and the instruments of its growth and expansion are not worldly. Wealth, intrigue, political glory and power, have no place within it. Some Jews, failing to understand this, had become disenchanted with the apparently plodding pace of heaven and determined to establish the rule of God by force (Matt 11.12). This mentality still lives, especially in those who are discontent with what the ways of the Lord are achieving, take the kingdom into their own presumptuous hands, and seek to accomplish by human guile what the grace and wisdom of the Almighty has failed in their minds to bring about. It can be seen in the carnal circus which many modern churches have become. These churches have their own agenda for "success" and they have taken up carnal instruments to achieve it.

It is not everyone that Jesus intends to draw to His kingdom. This is a hard fact to be faced. Jesus thanked the Father that He had hidden "these things from the wise and understanding, and revealed them to babes" (Matt 11.25), and then he called the "babes" to Him: "Come to me, all of you that labor and are heavy laden, and I will give you rest" (Matt 11.28).

These were the events, along with the Lord's subsequent conflicts with His critics among the scribes and Pharisees, which formed the backdrop for the preaching of the parables by the Sea. The first of them, the parable of the *Sower*, specifically addresses the question of why the kingdom of heaven sometimes grows so slowly, why its ways are not carnally spectacular, and why everyone who hears the call of the gospel does not respond. This illustration of the seed and the soils is not only a reproof of those who, losing confidence in the wisdom of heaven, would attempt to build the eternal kingdom on something other than the preaching of God's word, but it is also a great encouragement to those earnest souls whose evangelistic spirit have been sorely tried by what appears to be the constant rejection of the gospel. For them the temptation is to believe that there is some inadequacy in them, some failure of technique, some unskillful handling of the word. This very special parable says that it's not necessarily so, and urges every disciple to keep on preaching Christ with assurance and expectancy!

The Kingdom of Heaven Is Like a Farmer Sowing Seed

"Behold the sower went forth to sow…" (Matt 13.3).[1] It was an uncommon way for the Lord to open a discourse on the wonders of the kingdom of heaven. Could anything be more plodding and ordinary than a sower and his seed? How could something so unimaginative convey the glories of heaven's rule? His metaphor was so quiet. The coming of Messiah's reign would surely be explosive, sweeping, and cataclysmic. No, said Jesus, it will be more like a farmer sowing his field, and much of his seed going for nothing. Everything would depend upon the soil.

In all likelihood it would have been in the early spring of the year when Jesus took His seat in the prow of a fishing boat on the western shore of the Sea of Galilee and taught this remarkable parable. He would soon be on the eastern shore feeding a multitude of people with a few loaves and fishes (Matt 14.13–21), and the feast of Passover would be "at hand" (John 6.14). The fields that surrounded Geneseret would have been sown only a few months earlier (January, February). The smell of them would have been in the air and there would not be a man in the listening multitudes who did not know the weight of a bag of seed and the feel of freshly plowed soil. It was a land for farmers and husbandmen, a place for growing things, and the parable of the *Seed and the Soils* could not have found a more knowing audience.

The early spring light would have reflected how young the

---

[1] Of Jesus' first series of parables there are three accounts—Matthew 13, Mark 4, Luke 8. Four of these, likely five, the Lord addresses to the multitude (Matt 13.34): the Sower, the Tares, the Mustard Seed, Leaven, and one which Mark alone records, the Seed Growing Unobservedly (Mark 4.36–39). The remainder is spoken to the disciples alone (Matt 13.36–53).

teacher was, and perhaps how ordinary in appearance. In His eyes, in spite of the enthusiastic crowds that pressed upon Him, there may well have been a hint of sadness. They understood so little now, and most would never understand the gospel of His kingdom. And yet some would see. Some would always see. And that was the message of His story.

The people that pressed together to hear that day would have seemed of one mind to the less discerning. Had we been able to join them and take a closer look we would have discovered the differences. Some were doubtless listening with rapt attention, straining earnestly to catch every word. Others would have been seen to nod in mindless enthusiasm, carried away by the moment and the crowd. Still others would have been listening distractedly, hearing and agreeing, but with half a mind. And the scribes and Pharisees—they would have been listening, too—not to hear, of course, but to find the flaws and bore in on them.

Did Jesus know the thoughts that lay behind those faces? Did He know the prejudices, the justifying excuses, and the set ideas that were straining and filtering every word He spoke? Does He see the protective grids with which we shield our own hearts from His truth? He does—and warns us as He warned them, "He that hath ears, let him hear" (Matt 13.9).

"… **and as he sowed, some seeds fell by the way side, and the birds came and devoured them…**" (13.4). As to the disposition of this seed which fell on the wayside, Luke adds, "and was trodden under foot" (8.5).

The fields of Palestine were small and irregular, rimmed by narrow paths beaten into concrete by endless pounding feet. And often, as the farmer scattered his seed upon the freshly plowed soil with wide, regular sweeps of his hand, some would fall and dance upon the hard, unyielding surface of the "wayside" where all its rich potential ultimately became food for the birds.

This impenetrable soil in Jesus' story represents the hearers whose hearts are hard with willfulness and pride, hearts that have been made the high road of a thousand thundering passions, hearts that in their knowing compromise with evil cannot bear the pain of honesty. We think immediately of the Pharisees, and they were surely in the picture. Their arrogant, self-serving prejudices about the kingdom of God, their dreams of carnal splendor and power, made it impossible for them to see Jesus as the Messiah or hear His words as those of God. Many today follow in their train, so full of a 20th century caricature of Jesus that they cannot see the true Christ nor hear His real words.

But where does this steely resistance to the gospel of God's kingdom come from? What is it that causes people, even religious people, to become so hard against its gracious invitation? This rock-like rigidity begins to form the first time we learn to live easily with what we know is wrong. The hearing of every new truth is dependent upon the practice of the truth we already know. As John Ruskin once observed, every duty we omit will obscure some truth we might have known. Therefore, in our loathing to hear again the familiar truth we have not applied, we close our eyes and ears to the truth we yet need desperately to know.

"The Seed is the Word of God"

The curious multitude that heard the parable of the *Sower* did not understand it. But then, what did we expect? Neither did the Lord's disciples. "**Then Jesus said unto them, 'Haven't you understood this parable? How then will you understand any parable?'**" (Mark 4.13).

Jesus seems to have opened with the story of the Sower because it addressed so fundamental a concept of the kingdom of heaven that failure to understand it would portend failure to understand any. The salvation of the disciples was that though they truly didn't get His point, they wanted to, and stayed to ask further of His meaning and to listen to Jesus' patient explanation.

The parable of the *Sower* contains three elements: the sower, the seed, and the soils. The sower and the seed are constants. The sower is skilled and scatters the seed evenly. The seed is uniformly good. But the skillful labor of the sower and the germinating power of the seed all depend for their success on the nature of the soil, and here the parable is focused.

Who is the sower? Jesus does not say. In the parable of the *Wheat and the Tares* Jesus says that the sower of the good seed is the "Son of man" (Matt 13.37), but the concern in that parable is the contrasting origins of the two kinds of seed. Here the identity of the sower is not so critical. Who he might stand for is essentially a function of the purpose of the parable. If its intent was to illustrate the hearers' varying response to Jesus' personal preaching and to force them to serious self-examination, then almost surely the Lord is the sower. Jesus' application of the words of Isaiah to His audience, "For this people's heart is waxed gross, and their ears are dull of hearing and their eyes they have closed" (13.14–15) would seem to point in that direction.

But if, on the other hand, the purpose of this parable was also to strengthen the uncertain hearts of His disciples, expecting as they were the kingdom to carry every soul before it, then certainly they and those who would sow the world with the gospel after them would have to be part of this composite farmer.

The meaning of the seed is clearly marked out for us. "**Now the parable is this: The seed is the word of God**" (Luke 8.11). Though not the primary message of this parable, the fact that the word of God is the power which builds the kingdom of God needs emphasis.

There is no magic here, no mystifying esoteric energy. Even the words of men have power. They communicate feelings and ideas, create whole cultures, draw men to peace or war, change the course of history, and produce great evil or great good. Why should it surprise us, then, that the word of God should have power unimaginable?

The worlds were created and are upheld by the word of God (Heb 11.3; 1.3), and the divine breath that is in His words (Psa 33.6) is the breath that has given us life (Gen 2.7). The word of the Almighty fits and answers to our spirits like light answers to our eyes. Its powerful living truth pierces our hearts and lays bare our innermost thoughts (Heb 4.12). It is the word of the gospel that saves us (Rom 1.18; 1 Cor 1.21), and the "word of His grace" that builds us up and secures our inheritance among God's people (Acts 20.23).

This parable is telling us in plain language that the word of God is in and of itself the germinating seed of life (Phil 2.16), not the word plus some mysterious workings of the Holy Spirit. It is by this very living, energizing Word that the Holy Spirit not only brings us to spiritual rebirth (Eph 1.13; 1 Pet 1.23–25), but transforms us into the image of God's Son. And all this is possible because in His words God has opened up His heart to us and poured out the depths of His truth and grace (1 Cor 2.10–13). In the gospel He has made us look into the face of our crucified Savior (2 Cor 3.18). And that has power!

It is therefore sacrilege for men and women to speak of the gospel as "mere word" and laugh at the idea that the gospel alone is able to produce a new and unconquerable spiritual life. It is not wise to speak so lightly of the words that come out of the mouth of God or to insult heaven by attempting to fortify this "inadequate" word with our own vain philosophies (Col 2.8–10; Prov 30.5–6). Even Satan knows where the power is. "And those by the wayside are they that have heard; then comes the devil, *and takes away the word from their heart, that they may not believe and be saved*" (Luke 8.12).

But does not God do more than just speak to us? Yes, He is certainly active in answering our prayers (1 John 5.14–15), and providentially guiding us through the cleansing trials and tribulations that strengthen and purify our faith (Rom 8.28). But, at last, it is His word that has the power, and it is His word to which all His provident working must bring us, in understanding obedience. It is through that word that we come to know God and His Son. And that is eternal life (John 17.3). The seed of the kingdom is the word of God.

Counting the Cost

The parable of the *Sower* is a declaration of the inwardness of the kingdom of heaven. It is, as Jesus once said, a kingdom "within you" (Luke 17.20–21). The revolution is real, but it does not come "by observation." The reign of God enters only through the heart. It grows by seed and not sword and comes only to those who accept it humbly and gladly. Therefore, critical to its coming upon any human heart are new understandings and new resolves within.

In this is the mystery of God's ways with men. We are not privy to why He thought the joy of having people of His own, who loved Him and longed to be like Him, was worth the risk of the awful possibilities of sin and wickedness it opened up. In this, as in all other things, we are not able to sit in judgment on God. But He has surely limited Himself in creating us, for He cannot compel a single soul to do His will. Like any farmer, He plants His seed and waits patiently for the fruit of His labor; and however great and incredibly long His investment, it is still held hostage to the vagaries of the human heart, the soil into which He has lovingly cast His eternal word. And upon that soil the ultimate success or failure of all His efforts depend.

The Hard Heart

The hard hearts of the wayside soil produce absolutely nothing. These hearers live in a totally different world; do not speak the same language as the Son of God. Why would such people come to hear Jesus? Curiosity? Novelty? Fashion? Perhaps any or all. But they were not willing to truly listen to Him. Whether from smug self-satisfaction, or a prideful need to know everything already, or fear of exposure to some uncomfortable new truth about themselves, their minds were shut against the Lord and His gospel.

What is to be done with them? Nothing. They are hopeless in

their unyielding hardness. Only if God should plow a deep furrow of searing tragedy through their lives might some opening be given to the living seed. And if so, it would be a blessed pain.

The Shallow Heart

"**Some fell on rocky places, where it did not have much soil. It sprang up quickly because the soil was shallow. But when the sun came up, the plants were scorched, and they withered because they had no root**" (Matt 13.5–6). This was not earth mixed with countless small rocks, but soil which lay two or three inches deep upon a ledge of submerged stone. There was no place for the plant to root itself downward so it grew up lavishly, luxuriantly. But the heat of the sun revealed its unseen inadequacy. It flourished in the gentle times, but died away in the tough ones, unable to endure the very sunlight which with deeper roots would have made it even stronger. This soil, Jesus explained, was like the "man who hears the word and at once receives it with joy. But since he has not root, he lasts only a short time. When trouble or persecution comes because of the word, he quickly falls away" (Matt 13.20–21).

The shallow heart of the rocky soil is not like the hard heart of the wayside soil, steel-bound, rejecting the gospel with indifferent contempt, but these enthusiastic hearers are grievously lacking in careful forethought. Emotionally excitable and impulsive, they act upon immediate circumstances (the exciting crowds, etc.) more than upon an understanding of what is taught. They are heedless of future demands and challenges. They have entertained no long thoughts. The gospel has not gone down deeply into their understanding and will. So, when circumstances change, when the difficult days of persecution and adversity come, there is no profound root of faith to sustain them. They had not thought deeply of the kingdom and its ultimate, eternal worth. Becoming a disciple just seemed the thing to do at the time.

"**Immediately with joy....**" The shallow heart is passionate, but hasty. The gospel ought always to bring joy, but it needs a joy deep enough to withstand the shocks. It needs to be the kind of joy that time and circumstance cannot take away from us (John 16.22–24). It needs to be joy over the right thing (Luke 10.17), and it needs to be a joy that sees persecution and suffering for the sake of Christ as a privilege and a blessing (Luke 6.22–23). We must follow in the footsteps of our Lord "who for the joy that was set before him, endured the cross, despising the shame" (Heb 12.2). Becoming a Christian is certainly an emotional experience, but it is also an experience of the mind and the will.

This is the very reason that the one who comes too hastily to follow Jesus must stop and think about what that means. It is for our sake that the Lord often cools our heedless enthusiasm by warning us to stop a moment and count the cost (Luke 9.57–58). He wants us to go all the way with Him and not be derailed by some unanticipated hardship for a kingdom we have not come to value highly enough. My judgment is that nothing needs more to be taught to the average gospel prospect today, religious or non-religious, than the cost of discipleship. Those who come to the kingdom and survive must be deeply committed to Jesus.

The Crowded Heart

"And others fell upon the thorns; and the thorns grew up and choked them…" (Matt 13.7). This part of Jesus' story of the sower does not refer to seed sown in an already visible infestation of weeds, but in soil adulterated with the seeds of useless and burdensome plants. The soil is rich, deep, and receptive, but it is corrupted. The thorns, which will produce nothing good themselves, will simply grow up to burden the ground and sap the strength of the good seed until it, too, is fruitless. Of this thorn-possessed soil Jesus says, **"And he that was sown among the thorns, this is he that hears the word; and the care of the world and the deceitfulness of riches, choke the word and he becomes unfruitful"** (Matt 13.22). To the list of deterrents to fruitfulness, Mark adds "the lust of other things" (4.19), and Luke, "pleasures of this life" (8.14).

Some commentators, especially those of Calvinistic bent, dismiss this case as that of an unconverted heart—one that never received the word of the kingdom with fullness of spirit. This seems unlikely. In the unconverted no life is produced, the seed rots in the ground. Here there is not only life, but growth. The failure derives from what comes afterward—the rise of earthborn distractions which divide the heart and dissipate the energy of the soul.

The whole point of planted seed is not the growth of a plant, however luxuriant, but the production of fruit. The child of the kingdom of heaven is not just to look good, but to do good and to be good. The problem with the heart of the thorny soil is that it has become too crowded with competing concerns, and the seed of God cannot prosper in a divided heart.

What are the thorns that can bleed the spiritual vitality right out of a child of God? Jesus is explicit. The cares of this world can do it. Constant preoccupation with food and shelter and the fear of not having enough not only slanders God's faithfulness, but allows mindless anxiety to rob God of the energies we owe to Him (Matt 6.25–34). Christians who exhaust their powers in fear and worry will never blossom and bear fruit. Why do we kid ourselves? Worry is not only wasteful, it is sinful. It says implicitly that God will not help us and that we must muddle on without Him.

The love of things can also effectively suffocate the spirit. Money and property can seem so tangible, so real, and so securing; but riches are deceitful. They promise fulfillment and never give it (Ecc 5.9–10). They promise security, but fly off like a wild bird (Prov 23.5). We need to deal practically rather than emotionally with material things. We all know intellectually that they don't last. They are as ephemeral as a snowball in July. Why should a man be fool enough to build his life on sand? Still, many Christians think they can have their cake and eat it too. They only wind up as spiritual zombies who drag their emptiness to church assemblies and watch their children grow up to open worldliness without their parents' pious fraud. Such disciples are decorative plants. Don't expect anything lasting to come of them.

Finally, the "pleasures of this life" can work to suck us dry. "What's wrong with pleasures?" someone asks. "Is the life of the kingdom to be one long headache of misery and self-denial?" The answer to the first is "nothing," to the second "no." There is nothing wrong with working diligently for our food, or having wealth, or enjoying all the pleasant things which God has richly given us (1 Tim 6.17). But any or all of these things are wrong to those who have been "choked" by them, when they have become the passion of their lives. The Greek word translated "choked" in Luke 8.14 is later in the same chapter construed as "thronged" (8.42). Some people let these intrinsically legitimate things so overwhelm them that they are possessed and ruled by them. Legitimate concerns or blessings are then turned into fear, greed, and lust. God and His kingdom are crowded to the fringes. The voice of God becomes dim in the clamor. The blessings of our Father ought to be the occasion in His children for thanking Him and serving Him, but they can easily become the cause of our disaffection and uselessness.

Those who choose the divided heart, the crowded heart, says Jesus, will "bring no fruit to perfection" (Luke 8.14), literally, will never carry through to the end, will never finish the job.

We need be under no illusions about Jesus' attitude toward those who start but never finish. "No man, having put his hand to the plow, and looking back, is fit for the kingdom of God'" (Luke 9.62). We never need to wonder how He feels about the double-minded. "No man can serve two masters… . You cannot serve God and mammon" (Matt 6.24). And we certainly have no cause to doubt His feeling about the fruitless. "Every branch in me that bears no fruit, he takes it away…" (John 15.2). There is a future in God's kingdom for the single-minded, however fumbling—but for the divided heart, the crowded heart, there is no hope. "Purify your hearts, you double-minded" (Jas 4.8).

The True Heart

> And others fell upon the good ground, and yielded fruit, some a hundredfold, some sixty, some thirty. He that has ears, let him hear. ...And he that was sown upon the good ground, this is he that hears the word, and understands it; who verily bears fruit, and brings forth, some a hundredfold, some sixty, some thirty. (Matt 13.8–9, 23)

It is in the heart typified by good ground in the parable of the *Sower* that the spirit and character of the kingdom of heaven is captured and encompassed. It is here that the parable has its focus. The other soils—resistant, inadequate, and unproductive—tell us how to fail; the good soil tells us how to succeed.

In Luke's account Jesus identifies the seed sown in the good ground as those who receive "the word" with "an honest and good heart" (8.15). This description has nothing to do with essential righteousness, or even with the "good person," but with that attitude which the very sinfullest may have when confronted by the gospel. This is the heart, however wicked it may have been, which is now sincere, open, and devoid of all hypocrisy. As the Lord said, the call of His kingdom is not to the righteous but to sinners (Luke 5.32). And sinners can, if they choose, answer honestly.

This explanation will not content the Calvinist whose mistaken conviction that men are totally depraved and incapable of good makes his acceptance of this simple statement of Jesus impossible. False premises lead to false conclusions. Even wicked men and women can choose to have true hearts. The difference is that they will not continue to be wicked. As Jesus observed the religious elite in Jerusalem, "the publicans and harlots go into the kingdom of God before you" (Matt 21.31). The lives of publicans and prostitutes were undeniably and openly wicked, yet many of them dealt with themselves and the gospel honestly. The scribes and

Pharisees in their hypocrisy were honest neither with themselves nor the word of God. The gospel of the kingdom is a mirror (Jas 1.25) and a probe (Hebrews 4.12) that exposes the attitudes and motives of our hearts. "He that is of God hears the words of God," said Jesus (John 8.47), and, "Everyone that is of the truth hears my voice" (John 18.37).

In what ways is the "honest and good heart" good? In Matthew, the Lord says that they "hear the word and understand" (13.23). Mark records that they "hear the word and accept it" (4.20). The true heart then not only hears the word of the kingdom, but, unlike the hard heart (wayside soil), understands and receives it. All this makes clear that understanding God is not so much an intellectual exercise as it is a moral one. It is not too great an intellect that keeps men from the kingdom, but too small and unwilling a heart.

But there is more. Luke adds to the account that true hearts "having heard the word, hold it fast, and bring forth fruit with patience" (8.15). There is in the good heart, in contrast to the shallow heart (rocky soil), a dimension of depth and tenacity. In this mind there is a genuine comprehension of the worth of the kingdom and a willingness to suffer and invest patiently in order to possess it. Such a heart comes to know "the breadth and length and height and depth" of love and to be "filled with all the fullness of God" (Eph 3.18–19).

Finally, the "honest and good" hearts, unlike the crowded hearts (thorny ground), produce fruit that comes to harvest—that is, they fulfill God's purpose in their lives. What that "fruit" encompasses has been the subject of much discussion. Luke says that such hearts will all produce "a hundred fold" (8.8), or simply "bring forth fruit" (8.15).

Since it is God's purpose that His children be "conformed to the image of His Son" (Rom 8.29), the fruit to be borne must, at the least, refer to the fruit of the transformed life—the fruit of repentance (Matt 3.8), the "fruit of the Spirit" (Gal 5.22–23), "the peaceable fruit...of righteousness" (Heb 2.11), "the fruit of lips that make confession to His name" (Heb 13.15). Commenting on another verse in which Jesus speaks of the fruitfulness of His disciples (John 15.2), Hendriksen says, "These fruits are good motives, desires, attitudes, dispositions, words, deeds, all springing from faith, in harmony with God's law, and done to His glory" (*The Gospel of John*, p. 298). So we are not surprised to hear Paul refer to the way this fruit-filled heart abounds toward others in "bearing fruit in every good work" (Col 1.10), in mercy and compassion toward the needy (Rom 15.28) and in fellowship with those who preach the gospel (Phil 4.17).

Hearts Can Change

As Buttrick has observed, "No parable can be pressed to a rigorous conclusion. There is a point at which analogy ends." The soil of nature is not completely parallel to the "soil" of the heart. Natural soil has no power to alter its condition, but the heart can change. Happily, hard, shallow, and crowded hearts can become honest and good (Acts 8.22–23; Jas 4.8). And, unhappily, honest and good hearts can become hard, shallow, or divided (Heb 3.12–13). We need to be greatly sobered by the latter. By the former we can be greatly comforted, both as hearers and teachers of the gospel. The gospel of the kingdom is an appeal for hearts to change (Acts 3.19). What we have been does not determine what we can be. Sinners need to receive the grace of God with assurance, and Christians need to preach it with hope. Hearts that reject the gospel today are not necessarily lost causes. The word of God does not germinate in some hearts as quickly as others. We need, therefore, to learn how to patiently and lovingly water what we have planted and not be like the little girl who kept digging up the garden seed to see if anything was happening.

The heart of the woman Jesus met in Sychar of Samaria is almost a complete paradigm of all the hearts of the parable of the *Sower*. At first, she was hard and suspicious, "for Jews have no dealings with the Samaritans" (John 4.9). She had little sense of her own spiritual emptiness. But because she had come for water her heart opened up slightly when Jesus spoke of living water which would quench her thirst forever. "Sir, give me this water," she said, "that I thirst not, neither come hither to draw" (John 4.15). The Lord then plowed a deep furrow down her heart by asking her to go call her husband, thus reminding her of the wickedness of her life—five husbands and now just living with a man. She is struck, but her heart is crowded. Instead of facing her spiritual need forthrightly, she wanted to have a theological discussion about where men ought to worship in Jerusalem or Mt. Gerazim. By the time Jesus finished teaching her what it meant to truly worship God, she was profoundly caught. "I know that Messiah is coming," she said, and that "he will declare unto us all things" (John 4.25). "I that speak unto you am he," He replied; and the seed went home deeply and securely in the heart that had now turned absolutely honest. "And from that city many of the Samaritans believed on him because of the word of the woman, who testified, He told me all things whatsoever I did." She had been listening to the painful things He had told her about herself, and listening well. She had understood what a true worshipper of God was and that even she could be one. It changed her completely, and, as it must be, sent her out telling everyone who would listen how it happened and why. From every true heart comes much fruit, and what fruit this once hard and sinful, now earnest, woman bore!

But what is the meaning of the different yields from the good ground mentioned in Matthew and Mark, "**some a hundredfold, some sixty, some thirty**" (Matt 13.23)? Does this suggest differing degrees of faithfulness or consecration? This seems hardly likely. The heart of the good soil is absolutely single in contrast to the shallow heart of the rocky soil and the crowded heart of the thorny ground. If there is any lesson this parable teaches, it is that nothing less than total commitment is acceptable. What is more likely is that this parallels the parable of the *Talents* (Luke 19.16–19). Responsibility comes to us in the kingdom according to our ability. The fruit borne may vary, but the consecration of the heart does not. Surely the Lord will judge us by our opportunities and capacities, but a pure and single heart is the one thing that is non-negotiable.

And then, at last, the most obvious question for those who look seriously at the parables. What have I learned about myself? Which of the soils describes my attitude toward the Lord and His word? Is my commitment to Christ unstable, full of caprice and emotion? Does it struggle for life with the countless other competing interests of an overcrowded life? And if the answer is unsettling, what decision have I made to change?

Weeds in the Wheat:
The Parable of the Tares

The parables Jesus taught beside the Sea of Galilee (Matt 13, Luke 8, and Mark 4) were as much intended to define the kingdom of God as was the Sermon on the Mount. But His stories and comparisons had the opposite effect on those whose hearts had been stupefied by the worldly religion of the scribes and Pharisees. In the darkness of their understanding, the kingdom of heaven was even further mystified (Matt 13.11–15). The reason is, as Robert F. Capon has observed, the parables of Jesus set forth likenesses of the rule of heaven that made mincemeat of people's religious expectations. "Bad" people are rewarded. "Good" people are rebuked. And "in general, everybody's idea of who ought to be first or last is liberally doused with cold water" (*The Parables of the Kingdom*, p. 15).

But there is no greater mystery in the kingdom parables than the almost complete absence of emphasis on sheer divine power—absolute and immediate—the kind that would seem inseparable from the very idea of the rule of God. It is still the general belief that if God, who is not only completely righteous but also powerful, should establish a kingdom, it could only exist where all ungodliness is destroyed. If His kingdom is the reign of absolute righteousness, how can that kingdom be said in any sense to exist where unrighteousness not only seems to be present, but even to prevail? This question is really just an extension of a more fundamental issue which has perplexed men for ages—how can there be evil in a world ruled by a good God? For some it is simple. If God wants to set up His kingdom, what's the need for delay? He's got the power. Why doesn't He just knock heads, throw the rascals out, and make everything beautiful?

And then there is a second and similar question which many, Trench among them, believe to be the issue dealt with in this parable. How can the kingdom of heaven be real if there exists within it all kinds of sham and hypocrisy?

Although there is considerable controversy about which of the above stated questions Jesus' parable of the *Tares* addresses, there can hardly be any serious doubt that it speaks to one or the other of them. Found only in Matthew (13.24–30, 36–43), the story of the tares sown in the field follows immediately upon the parable of the *Sower*. In the parable of the *Sower*, Jesus has already intimated that righteousness (the good soil) will have to flourish in a world where many reject the kingdom of God (the wayside soil) and others receive it in a shallow and unfruitful way (rocky and thorny soil). In the story of the *Tares*, He seems to pick up where He left off in the *Sower* and make explicit what was earlier only suggested. The kingdom of heaven is indeed destined to grow up and make its way in the heart of a world where evil is not only very much alive and active, but will continue to be until that world ends. To say the least, this is a surprise, and for many, an incredible shock. It is 180 degrees out of phase with most people's idea of the kingdom of heaven. For them the kingdom of heaven has not come until all ungodliness is blasted away, all evil removed, and unbroken peace and safety established. The kingdom is to come by the paradox of what Luther called the "left-handed power" of God—giving to gain, losing to win, and dying to live.

> Another parable He set before them, saying, The kingdom of heaven is likened unto a man that sowed good seed in his field: but while men slept, his enemy came and sowed tares among the wheat, and went away. But when the blade sprang up and brought forth fruit, then appeared the tares also. (Matt 13.24–26)

Our immediate reaction to this parable might be, "What kind of farmer is this—careless about keeping weeds out of his field, sleeping when he should have been alert?" But the farmer of this parable is not a negligent man who has made no effort to keep his ground free of weeds, or who has slept away his days when he should have been conscientious. His wheat crop is strong. He has slept only as hardworking men sleep—at night. The problem is that *he has an enemy* who will stop at nothing to destroy what he had no part or interest in planting in the first place. The weeds are not discovered early because *they were not expected* and the weeds sown are so like wheat when in the blade that their masquerade was not discovered until they began to head out. The tares (Greek *zizanion*, specifically darnel, Lolium temulentum), were an annual grass which looked very much like wheat until it matured. Arndt and Gingrich define it as "darnel, cheat, a troublesome weed in the grain fields, resembling wheat" (p. 340). Thayer says that it is "a kind of darnel, bastard wheat, and resembling wheat except that its grains are black" (p. 272).

So why were these troublesome weeds not to be removed immediately? Not because they were not sapping the ground, burdening the soil, and challenging the wheat for nourishment, and not because they were not now easily identifiable, but because any effort to root out the weeds, now grown up and securely rooted and mingled with the wheat, would have uprooted the wheat as well. Wait, the farmer said to his servants, "until the harvest."

The Challenge of Small Beginnings

> Another parable spake he unto them, saying, the kingdom of heaven is like unto a grain of mustard seed, which a man took, and sowed in his field; which indeed is less than all seeds, but when it is grown, it is greater than the herbs, and becometh a tree, so that the birds of the heaven come and lodge in the branches thereof. (Matt 13.31–32)

One of the greatest mistakes of amateur landscapers is the failure to anticipate how great a tree can grow from a very small sapling. So it is with those who see the inconsiderable beginning of the kingdom of God and judge that it will always be a matter of little consequence. For, as we well know, it is not the size of the seed that determines what it will at last become, but the living germ within it. It is this truth which Jesus uses to illustrate the true destiny of a kingdom that will have a very inauspicious beginning, but will in the end overwhelm the world. This is certainly the message which one-dimensional, carnally-minded men need to hear, but it is also the comforting word needed by the Lord's disciples who have just been warned in the parables of the *Sower* and the *Tares* that the kingdom of heaven, far from being universally received, will have to grow up amidst evil forces which will try mightily to destroy it. This was certainly not the kingdom of popular expectation, not even among Jesus' most intimate disciples.

The mustard seed was the proverbial symbol of smallness in the ancient Jewish world (Matt 17.20). In this parable Jesus notes how the kingdom of God is like that tiny, seemingly inconsequential seed, which will in time grow to be a tree large enough to shelter the birds. The parable is not in the size of the mustard plant. Even though it evidently grew to remarkable size for an herb in ancient Palestine, it would obviously not compare to those great trees which are used at times in the Scripture as symbols of mighty kingdoms (Ezek 17.24; Dan 4.20–22). The parable focuses instead upon the immense difference between the tiny seed and the plant which rises out of it.

The kingdom of heaven did indeed begin unimpressively. That is illustrated by the exceedingly humble birth of its king who began His life in a Palestinian stable, the child of an obscure Jewish peasant girl with nothing to her credit save her remarkable piety and faith. And that which began so unimpressively did not later explode in heavenly glory. The child grew up to be a penniless teacher without educational, social, or political credentials. How truly Isaiah said of Him, "he has no form or comeliness; and when we see him, there is no beauty that we should desire him" (53.2).

The one thing most to be expected and most absent from this kingdom was the presence of overwhelming heavenly power. Power came, but in muted, gentle forms—the healing of the sick and raising of the dead. There was nothing that would force the ungodly immediately to their knees or pull down wicked powers. The demonstration of divine power that came seemed largely intended to simply call attention to the Teacher and His message; to move people to listen, to learn, and to follow Him gladly (John 20.30–31; Heb 2.3–4). Jesus did for a time attain some celebrity and a popular following among His countrymen, but at last they turned on Him viciously, murdering Him without a backward glance. One would have to wonder what sort of a kingdom it is that begins like that.

And that is exactly what John the Baptist did, even before it all seemed to end with Jesus' death. He sent his disciples to Jesus with the question, "Are you the one to come or shall we look for another?" (Matt 11.3). How could John the Baptist ask such a question? He had himself heard the voice of God thunder His testimony from heaven, "This is my beloved Son, in whom I am well pleased" (Matt 3.17). He had declared Jesus to be "the Lamb of God who takes away the sin of the world" (John 1.29).

Perhaps the explanation lies in the fact that this free spirit of the wilderness who had heralded the impending appearance of the kingdom of God was now suffocating in Herod's prison. He had by his preaching filled the Judean wilderness with people, their expectations at a fever pitch, and now this! Why should we wonder that John, like the disciples of Jesus, had dreams of an immediate heavenly cataclysm and the ultimate victory of God? It is important to remember that the one in whose spirit John the Baptist came, had also once been driven into deep depression by the shocking reversal of events that followed his great victory at Mt. Carmel (1 Kgs 19). Jesus answered John gently, but firmly. "Go and tell John the things which you hear and see: the blind receive their sight and the lame walk, the lepers are cleansed, and the deaf hear, and the dead are raised up, and the poor have good tidings preached to them. And blessed is he, whomsoever shall find no occasion of stumbling in me" (Matt 11.4–6).

The Lord does not promise John greater things soon to come or myriad angels bursting forth from heaven to make everything right. There were only to be the healing wonders and the preaching of the gospel to the poor, the very signs that Isaiah had said would herald the arrival of heaven's kingdom (Isa 35.5–6; 61.1). And blessed, He said, are those who find no disappointment in Him or in His kingdom.

Heaven's Kingdom:
How Large A Tree?

In Luke's account of the parable of the *Mustard Seed*, Jesus says that the mustard seed "grew and became a tree..." (Luke 13.19). We have already observed that this parable stresses more the contrast between seed and plant than the immensity of its final growth. As A.B. Bruce has observed, the parable seems to more emphasize the smallness of the kingdom's beginning than the greatness of its end. However large a tree a mustard seed may grow to be, it will never rival the true trees which tower over it. The companion parables of the *Mustard Seed* and the *Leaven* both seem intended to illustrate the future growth and influence of the kingdom. One speaks to its extensive, visible growth, the other to intensive spiritual change. But the question that remains is whether Jesus is looking in the parable of the *Mustard Seed* at the final victorious destiny of His kingdom or simply at the enlarging visible and spiritual influence of the gospel in history.

The prophets spoke eloquently of the absolute and final triumph of the Messianic kingdom. Isaiah foresees the "mountain of the Lord's house" as "established in the top of the mountains" and "exalted above the hills" (2.2). Daniel says that the kingdom will become a great mountain and fill the whole earth (2.35) and that the dominion of its King will be "an everlasting dominion which shall not pass away" (7.14). But Jesus' choice of the mustard tree for an illustration of the kingdom's future seems an unlikely metaphor with which to describe its final glory. Perhaps it was purposefully chosen to emphasize the great spiritual influence which the kingdom of God would wield in the world and in history despite its small beginning, and yet give His disciples no visions of worldly glory. Within the span of their generation, the gospel was to be preached "in all creation under heaven" (Col 1.23) and to touch the hearts of men from Jerusalem to "the uttermost part of the earth" (Acts 1.8). But is the mustard tree intended to speak of the growth of the church into an institution of such great worldly power that the society of ungodly men will tremble before it? That view seems more in tune with Roman Catholic theology or premillennial speculations. What the preceding parables of the *Sower* and the *Tares* have already clearly said is that the kingdom of heaven is destined to be rejected by the vast majority of men and to be at war with the children of the devil as long as the world stands. There is no room in these parables for the church of God to rule supreme in some new-age Holy Roman Empire or to preside over the absolute righteousness and peace of an earthly millennium. There will doubtless be times when the gospel is more "in season" than in others (2 Tim 4.2), but such times of peace and greater advance (Acts 9.31) are likely always to be followed by periods of opposition, retrenchment, and apostasy (1 Tim 4.1; 2 Tim 3.1–5; 4.3–4). Righteous people are never destined to escape persecution in this life (2 Tim 3.12).

The parable of the *Tares* tells us plainly that the time of final glory and triumph for the kingdom will come "at the end of the world" (Matt 13.39) when "the Son of Man shall send forth His angels, and they shall gather out of his kingdom [all men living and dead, Rom 14.9, PE] all things that cause stumbling, and them that do iniquity" (Matt 13.41). It will be, then, and not before, at the same time that the wicked are cast into the furnace of fire, that "the righteous shall shine forth as the sun in the kingdom of their Father" (Matt 13.42–43). It will be then that the kingdom of God fills the whole earth, and the Lord and His Anointed, always having absolute sovereignty, will hold the kings of the earth in final and complete derision, and dash them like a potter's vessel (Psa 2).

It is the Lord's way to work His wonders by means of the most humble of people and circumstances and so to make evident that only God could have brought them to pass. Paul says of the gospel that "God chose the weak things of the world that he might put to shame the things that are strong.... that no flesh should glory before God" (1 Cor 1.27, 29). So it seems to me that the day will never come when God's people find themselves happily in a position of worldly glory without being corrupted by their very success. It is by the difficulties that Christians are called to endure that the Lord assures that only the true of heart will come. The Lord led Israel across a trackless waste with nothing but His promise to sustain them so that in their need He might know what was in their hearts and they might know that man does not live by bread alone, but by the word of God (Deut 8.2–3). We will likely always be the "little flock" (Luke 12.32) sent out by the Lord "like sheep in the midst of wolves" (Matt 10.16) so that we will trust in Him alone.

Meanwhile, the kingdom of heaven will always be a tree large enough to shelter every true and penitent heart that seeks refuge in its Lord, and a tree sufficiently devoid of worldly attraction as to hold no charms for the carrion eaters who might seek shelter in its branches for their own dark and carnal reasons.

Parable of the Leaven:
The Heavenly Contagion

> Another parable he spoke to them; the kingdom of heaven is like leaven, which a woman took, and hid in three measures of meal, till it was all leavened. (Matt 13.34; see also Luke 13.20–21)

Of all the parables which Jesus taught beside the Sea of Galilee, this is the briefest. It ends almost as quickly as it begins, leaving us to grapple with its quick, incisive message. Both Matthew and Luke record this parable in immediate association with the parable of the *Mustard Seed*, which leaves with the clear impression that it, too, has to do with the way the kingdom expands, although its thrust seems more inward than outward.

"The kingdom of heaven is like leaven…." In the Law of Moses, leaven was, with a few exceptions, forbidden in offerings, and during the Passover all leaven was to be removed from the house (Exod 13.3; Lev 2.11; Amos 4.5). In every other case in the New Testament where leaven is used as a figure, it is used of an evil influence (Luke 12.1; 1 Cor 5.7; Gal 5.9). For this reason some have concluded that the leaven in this parable symbolizes a malevolent force, the stealthy coming in of apostasy (J. N. Darby, *Brief Exposition of Matthew*, 1845, p. 40). But the parable of the *Leaven*, like all others in the series by the Sea, is explicitly said to depict the kingdom of heaven, not the rule of Satan (Matt 13.33; Luke 13.20–21). There is no real problem here since all spiritual influence, both evil and good, works in the same fashion, and differing usage of the same metaphor is not unknown in the Scriptures. Both Satan and Christ are compared to a lion (1 Pet 5.8; Rev 5.5); but in the devil is seen the lion's ruthless stalking of his prey, and in Jesus his strength and courage. The dove in one place is used to illustrate silliness (Hos 7.11) and in another, harmless simplicity (Matt 10.16).

"Which a woman hid in three measures of meal...." As Buttrick has observed, "This parable has suffered many offences at the hands of allegorizers." Some have seen in the woman either the church or the Holy Spirit when nothing more seems intended than that this is the kind of work customarily done by women. To Augustine the three measures of meal represented the whole human race in the three sons of Noah; to Jerome and Ambrose they signified the sanctification of spirit, soul, and body. Though these ideas may not in general be far off from the significance of the meal, the three measures in all likelihood simply suggest nothing more than the customary amount of dough used in the ancient world in baking bread (i.e., about a bushel, Gen 18.6; Jdg 6.19; 1 Sam 1.24).

The parable of the *Leaven* seems to speak to the quiet inner transformation which the kingdom of God works in the human spirit and the unostentatious way it moves from heart to heart. So leaven, like light and salt (Matt 5.13–14), is a quiet but powerful agency. In just such a way Jesus worked among men: "He shall not strive nor cry aloud nor lift up his voice in the streets" (Isa 42.2–3; Matt 12.17–21). Yet His work was never secretive or stealthy: "I have spoken openly to the world; I always taught in synagogues and in the temple, where the Jews always meet, and in secret I have said nothing" (John 18.20).

The work of leaven is also inward and invisible. This parable is a powerful declaration of the spiritual nature of the kingdom. It was this very point Jesus once made to the Pharisees: "The kingdom of God does not come with observation: neither shall they say, Lo, here! or, There! for lo, the kingdom of God is within you" (Luke 17.20–21). The radical revolution of the kingdom of Christ (unlike the kingdoms of men, John 8.36) was to explode quietly within, working a complete transformation of the heart. The leaven must therefore symbolize the gospel as it works unseen in the individual spirit (1 Pet 1.22–23) and then moves quietly from one heart to another (Acts 8.4).

The word of God is the germinating seed from which the new life of God comes, but those who have been touched by it also become light, salt, and leaven in the world (Matt 5.13–14; Phil 2.15).

Their humility of spirit and godliness of life "adorn the doctrine of God" (Tit 2.10) and inevitably attract and then infect others with the same powerful heavenly contagion that has changed their own lives. The movement of such a profound spiritual force is not noisy or clamorous like an army on the march, but steady, quiet and inexorable like the tender plant that first penetrates, then cracks, and finally bursts the most obdurate of rocks.

"**Till it all was leavened....**" If we are to understand by the dough the heart of a single soul, then it is right to take the "all" as an absolute because in Christ everything is made new (2 Cor 5.17); the whole of the personality is penetrated. But if the dough symbolizes the world, the parable must be understood to speak of the leavening of every honest and good heart and not of universal salvation (Matt 7.13–14), or some universal social influence or an unconverted humanity. It is inconceivable that the one who came to "seek and save that which is lost" should ever concern Himself with the mere social impact of the gospel. With Jesus and His kingdom it was personal redemption, or nothing (John 3.3–5).

All Things New

The parable of the *Leaven* reminds us that God sent His Son into the world not only to forgive but to transform. So immense a thing as the cross was never intended merely to provide mercy for our sinful past while leaving us the same proud, selfish, and lustful individuals we were before. We are to be changed, and about that transformation this little parable tells us much.

First of all, it is a transformation that must come from without. Archimedes, the Greek who discovered the principle of the lever, once observed, "Give me a place to stand, and I will move the world." That is the problem. The "world" desperately needs to be moved, but we have no place to stand outside it. The leaven of renewal is beyond human power and all self-help systems are doomed by definition. We are as incapable alone of reshaping our lives after the righteousness of God as we are of escaping the just judgment of God for our sins. Only heaven's fire is powerful enough to effect such a radical change. By God's grace we have been forgiven, and it is by His grace and power that we will at last be wholly renewed (Eph 2.8–10; 3.14–21).

Secondly, it is a transformation which must be worked within. Much modern political and even religious thinking rests on the often discredited myth that man is shaped by his environment and that changing his circumstances will change his heart. Truth lies in the very opposite direction. "Keep your heart with all diligence," warns Solomon, "for out of it spring the issues of life" (Prov 4.23). Life, whether good or ill, springs from the mind, and new life can come only from a heart that has been persuaded in new directions. Therefore, like yeast in bread dough, the kingdom of heaven directs its attack inward, upon the heart.

External change made apart from internal revolution is mere accommodation (Rom 12.2), and its shallowness robs it of staying power. It will fade in the face of the least inconvenience. In contrast, external change effected by a changed heart is true transformation and its depth gives it a dogged immovability (1 Cor 15.58). This kind of conversion not only resists control from without but exercises a profound and positive influence on others. The heart is critical. In a parable titled "The Holocaust," Nathaniel Hawthorne pictures a bonfire where men are burning up all the evil things of the world. Satan, looking on, is at first dismayed, but then he brightens and observes, "I am not done yet. They have forgotten to throw in the human heart." This is the reason that inherited second-hand religiosity, however true in form, will always lack reality and power (2 Tim 3.5). The lump will never be leavened. The life will never be truly transformed.

Thirdly, it is a transformation which must touch the whole of our lives. Not the tiniest segment can be excluded, because in that narrow sliver will hide our will and our way. It has never been otherwise. God has always required that men love and serve Him in the wholeness of their hearts (Deut 6.4; 11.13; 13.3; Jer 29.13).

In the final analysis it is Christ who is the leaven. Christ crucified, yes, and truly the Christ of the Scriptures, but still Christ the person moving personally by the influence of His remarkable character and will into every recess of our hearts. Paul defined the riches and glory of the gospel mystery when he said that it is "Christ in you, the hope of glory" (Col 1.27). The leaven of the Son of God enters our lives when we accept not only His love and forgiveness, but also His lordship. There is enormous personal power in the knowledge that He has no intention of leaving us there.

Our lives are changed by looking intently upon the glory that is Jesus (2 Cor 3.18). There are two things we will see by looking into the face of Christ. First of all, what we are not. Never do men know how deep their wickedness has been until they look with honesty into the face of absolute holiness and righteousness, and that not lived out in heavenly isolation but in the grimy reality of human flesh. It is a dismaying experience, but one absolutely necessary to our transformation. How can we ever be different until we know how desperately we need to be?

The second thing we will see in the face of Jesus is what we can be. However much His holiness has made us see our own impurity, His love will at the same time fill us with a vision of what His grace and power can make us. We are to be "transformed into the same image from glory to glory, just as by the Spirit of the Lord" (2 Cor 3.18).

And at last what Christ has been in us as the yeast of eternity, always enlarging, expanding, changing us, we must be in the world. People will be able to see what can happen to them by observing what has happened to us (Matt 5.13–16).

> "Let the beauty of Jesus be seen in me,
> All His wonderful passion and purity,
> May His spirit divine all my being refine,
> Let the beauty of Jesus be seen in me."

Possessing the Priceless

> Again, the kingdom of heaven is like treasure hidden in a field, which a man found and hid; and for joy over it he goes and sells all that he has and buys that field. (Matt 13.44)

The parables of the *Hidden Treasure* and the *Pearl of Great Price* are recorded only by Matthew. Along with the parable of the *Dragnet* they make up the concluding trio of parables with which Jesus closes His series on the nature of the kingdom of heaven. Unlike the earlier parables, addressed to the multitude, these were evidently spoken privately to His disciples.

The two parables contain the same message—the incomparable worth of the kingdom of God. But each parable has its own unique way of delivering its lesson and deserves at least some individual treatment.

The only real dispute about the meaning of these two parables which would radically affect their message is over what Jesus meant in them by "the kingdom." There are those who take the view that the farmer and the merchant in these two stories is Christ (Lloyd John Ogilvie, *The Autobiography of God*), and that the "hid treasure" and "pearl of great price" represent the church, whose redemption from sin literally cost Him everything, a price He joyfully paid. There is no disputing the truth of such an idea, but the question is whether that is the message of these parables.

The Greek word *baseleia* (kingdom) certainly includes by implication those ruled over, but its root idea is the power and dominion of the king. The worth of the kingdom of heaven does not rest principally in those who by divine grace have been permitted to receive it, but in the glory and power of the God who reigns over it. Jesus' parables of the kingdom have all spoken to this point of how the kingdom grows. Nothing in the context of these two parables would suggest that in them Jesus has turned His attention away from how He would establish His reign among men, to the great value He has placed upon lost men and women. It is a valid point made powerfully in other places, but not, we believe, here.

In the late twentieth century talk of buried treasure calls to mind semi-legendary nonsense about pirate booty hidden away in some island cove where it awaits retrieval by the fortunate. But in first century Palestine it was not nearly so far-fetched. The disorder which wars and revolutions regularly imposed on the oriental world made it necessary for men to bury valuables they could not safely carry with them when forced to flee for their lives. Sometimes they never got back to claim their hidden property and the land passed to those who had no knowledge of what was buried beneath it. The Bible refers to the practice. The assassin who killed the Chaldean governor of Judah spared the lives of ten men in order to obtain the rich store of goods they claimed to have hidden in a field (Jer 41.8). It was also the basis of a common metaphor in the ancient world. Job spoke of those who searched for death "more than hidden treasures" (Job 3.21) and Solomon urges young men to search for wisdom "as for hidden treasures…" (Prov 2.4).

The man in Jesus' story who quite accidentally finds a very valuable treasure buried in a field was clearly not on a treasure hunt. He was most likely simply plowing another man's ground when the plow struck and exposed something that was neither rock nor stump. Incredulous at his good fortune, heart pounding with excitement, the man quickly reburies his find and goes fairly bursting with secret joy and sells everything he has to buy the field. One can well imagine that all his friends and neighbors must have thought him entirely mad, selling all his cherished possessions to buy a field not worth half he was paying for it and laughing delightedly as everything he owned went on the block. Human nature being what it is, they probably told him plainly that he was crazy as a loon and may well have tried to forcibly restrain him from his folly. But absolutely nothing could deter him, not ridicule, not threats, not abuse; because he had seen and knew that the treasure hidden in that field was worth everything he had and a hundred times more.

The kingdom of heaven is like that, Jesus said, a treasure so fabulously great that it is worth everything a man owns, every relationship he ever had or hopes to have, even his very own life (Matt 10.37–39; Luke 14.25–26). Those who find the heavenly kingdom will likely be thought mad by the unknowing. George Bernard Shaw is reported to have said that he knew there was life in outer space because they were using the earth for an insane asylum! It is not easy being sane in a madhouse, but when you know the eternal worth of what you have found in Christ, all others notwithstanding, the joy of that confidence will surely carry you through the hardest of losses without the slightest regret. That is the "joy unspeakable and full of glory" which comes from discovering what life is all about, the treasure that is worth all others.

Finding the Ultimate

> Again, the kingdom of heaven is like a merchant seeking beautiful pearls, who, when he had found one pearl of great price, went and sold all that he had, and bought it. (Matt 13.45–46)

The ancients considered pearls to be extremely precious and were as fascinated with them as moderns are with large diamonds. Mysterious explanations were given of their formation and fabulous sums were paid to possess them. For this reason merchants of ancient times scoured the world for the most beautiful specimens and, consequently, provided for Jesus a most compelling illustration of the search for the ultimate, the highest good.

The message of the parable of *Great Price* and that of the treasure hidden in the field is clearly the same. The men in both parables recognize the worth of what they have found and do not hesitate to sell all they have to possess it. Neither has to be cajoled or wheedled into action. They move with joyful abandon. So, says Jesus, is the kingdom of heaven. It costs all we possess but it is the highest good, the incomparable treasure and the joy of obtaining it will overwhelm any sense of loss.

The cost of discipleship was a frequent theme with the Lord. He wanted no disillusionment (Luke 9.57–62). His language was often graphic. "If anyone comes to me and does not hate his father and mother, wife and children, brothers and sisters, yes, and his own life also, he cannot be my disciple" (Luke 14.26). Such statements were the practical expression of His demand for absolute loyalty. Those who followed Him had to be prepared to give up everything for His sake (Matt 16.24–25).

How is it, someone asks, that a kingdom given by God's grace has to be bought at so dear a price? First of all, the incomparable worth of the kingdom of Heaven puts it beyond purchase. When sinful people are given by God what they have absolutely no right to and no ability to obtain, it has to be a gift. But, by definition, the gift of the kingdom or reign of God cannot be possessed by those who will not yield themselves wholly to Him. The price we pay to be the followers of Christ is not in things but in our overriding affection for them; not in people but in our preeminent commitment to them; and not in position or pleasure but in our primary love of them. The kingdom of Christ is found where "Christ is all in all" (Col 3.11). All that we are and have must be made to serve Him.

But if Jesus in these two parables speaks of the cost of the kingdom, it is not their primary thrust. Our Lord does not call us by the cost of discipleship but by the transcendent joys of following Him. You cannot persuade a man to set fire to his house by telling Him how wretched it is. If it is a pigsty, it is the only one he has. But if you give him assurance of something far better, he will gladly burn it and dance around the flames. The two men of these parables do not give up everything out of some perverse asceticism but because they have found something so superior that it makes what they have now seem as nothing. So Paul's casting away as garbage everything he formerly cherished was not a teeth gritting exercise in self-denial, but a reaction to the transcendent worth of Christ (Phil 3.8–10). As he wrote so powerfully in Colossians, "Christ is all" (3.11), "the fullness of the Godhead bodily" (2.9), the one "in whom are hidden all the treasures of wisdom and knowledge" (2.3). When men truly see "the glory of God in the face of Jesus Christ" (2 Cor 4.6), they can never again be content with this world's smoke and mirrors. "He is no fool who gives what he cannot keep to gain what he cannot lose."

But, as earlier noted, there is some dissimilarity in these two similar parables. The man who found the hidden treasure discovered it wholly by accident. He was "surprised by joy." The merchant, on the other hand, was on a serious quest. If there was any surprise for him, it was that he found what he was looking for in one pearl alone. We often wonder where we can find prospects for the kingdom. These two parables tell us the answer. They will appear in earnest souls like the Ethiopian noblemen or the Italian soldier, Cornelius, who are knowingly looking for the kingdom. And they will be found among those like the Samaritan woman whose lives are occupied with the mundane and immoral and give no sign of spiritual concern. These await only the concerned approach of a disciple of the One who came to seek and to save the lost.

Troublesome Kingdom of "Every Kind"

> Again, the kingdom of heaven is like a dragnet that was cast into the sea and gathered some of every kind, which, when it was full, they drew to shore; and they sat down and gathered the good into vessels but threw the bad away. So it shall be at the end of the age. The angels will come forth, separate the wicked from among the just, and cast them into the furnace of fire. There will be wailing and gnashing of teeth. (Matt 13.46–50, NKJV)

In the parable of the *Dragnet*, Jesus draws upon another familiar image of the work-a-day Palestinian world, one that would have been especially common around the Sea of Galilee. The dragnet was a very large fishing net, weighted on one side and floated on the other which, when dragged from the deep water to the shore brought up in its meshes every creature in the water. Obviously, all would not be useful for food, especially among the Jews, and everything unsuitable had to be removed. Jesus says that in some particulars the kingdom of heaven is like that dragnet.

This last of the seven Parables by the Sea recorded by Matthew is usually linked closely with the parable of the *Tares* and given a similar interpretation. As straightforward as these parables seem to be, they have been the source of much controversy. The reason is that they appear to reject any exercise of spiritual discipline by the church against unruly disciples; no judgment of the rightness or wrongness of the behavior of Christians being made before the final judgment. This is especially the case with the parable of the *Tares*. Luther resolved this problem by arguing that the efforts to remove the ungodly from the church were only prohibited when one might also dislodge the true children of the kingdom. But this jars against the fact that the farmer's order to his workers not to remove the tares is unconditional (Matt 13.29–30). The interpretive flaw lies in understanding the field in the parable to be the church rather than the world. We have already indicated our belief that the parable of the *Tares* is not dealing with church discipline at all but with the then surprising fact that the kingdom of heaven was to exist for a time in the midst of an ungodly and inhospitable world ("the field is the world," 13.38). The judgment under consideration is not corrective discipline, but final or ultimate judgment, a judgment which only the divine mind has the right or capability to make (1 Cor 4.3–5).

Those who oppose this view make much of Jesus' statement that the angels will "gather *out of his kingdom* all things that cause stumbling..." (Matt 13.41). But the meaning of *His kingdom* must be understood in its context. The *kingdom* does often speak of the church, but at times it takes in the total sphere of the Lord's sovereign rule, even those who are in rebellion (Luke 19.14–15, 27; see Eph 1.20–23). We believe that such is the case in the parable of the *Tares*. The kingdom of heaven was destined to bring not immediate peace and triumph but tribulation (Rev 1.9; Acts 14.22; Matt 5.10; John 16.33; 2 Tim 3.12). By this parable, citizens of the kingdom are urged to wait patiently for their vindication in the glory of the final righteous judgment of the Almighty. It is a parable of comfort and encouragement to rejected and suffering saints.

But that is not the case with the parable of the *Dragnet*. This is a dark and dreadful parable, a parable of judgment and rejection. Chrysostom called it "a terrible parable." Further, what we have denied of the parable of the *Tares*, we believe to be true of this parable, that it addresses the character of the church rather than the world at large, and that it speaks to the ultimate purification of the fellowship of the saints. Those taken by the dragnet in this parable do not represent all men but those specifically drawn in by the gospel. So what may not be taught by the parable of the *Tares* is certainly taught here. Until God acts in final judgment, there will be mixed among the righteous of the kingdom those who are "wicked."

This is a difficult message to accept. Is this what Jesus is saying? Does this mean that local churches cannot completely exclude the unfaithful and unholy from their number? Is the common charge that the church is a hotbed of hypocrisy just to be accepted as inevitability? Are we destined to have to live easily in the kingdom with all sorts of heresy and immorality? It is just such questions as these which our study of this parable must answer.

The Parable of the Dragnet:
Pure At Last!

While the parable of the *Tares* might be suspected of speaking to the question of church discipline (though we are strongly persuaded it does not), no such possibility exists with the parable of the *Dragnet*. It speaks solely to the final removal from the kingdom all that are not true disciples. The kingdom of God will not always be a place where impure motives, dark lusts, and spiritual half-heartedness can conceal themselves amidst the righteous, but will at last be cleansed of all that is unholy. The cast-away fish of the parable are the "wicked," and those who remove them are "angels," and the time is "the end of the world." The purpose of the purging of the net is not redemptive. The rejection is final. The judgment is divine.

The ideal image of the heavenly kingdom is seen in the parables of the *Hidden Treasure* and the *Pearl of Great Price*. In these parables all who become a part of the kingdom do so at the level of absolute devotion. All things are yielded to the rule of Christ. But the reality is that many attach themselves to the kingdom who are not totally committed or not committed at all. The parable of the *Sower* makes this evident. Of those who receive the gospel, some will be shallow and others will be half-hearted (the rocky soil and thorny ground). There are several illustrations of this truth in the New Testament—the church at Corinth with its immorality and carnal divisiveness, the churches of Galatia with their Judaizing teachers of righteousness by the law, the churches to whom John wrote his epistles with their gnostic prophets of a new and improved gospel, and five of the seven churches of Asia plagued variously with idolatry, immorality, false teaching, lovelessness, and smug complacency. As for the present, it does not take much observation in twentieth-century churches of the Lord to learn that things have not changed. We are still troubled, not simply with the momentary weakness or ignorance of those who are making their journey to spiritual maturity, but with entrenched worldliness and pride and a knowing determination to corrupt the doctrine of Christ.

It may be rightly objected that in the New Testament such spiritual aberrations in churches or individual saints were not accepted with resignation. Paul urged the church in Corinth to get its spiritual house in order (1 Cor 1.10), to have no company with those Christians who were determined to practice ungodly ways (5.11–13). In fact, he says, using the very Greek word chosen by Matthew to record the parable of the *Dragnet* ("the wicked," *ponerous*), "put away from yourselves the evil person [*poneron*]." The Judaizing teachers troubling the churches of Galatia were anathematized by Paul as perverters of the gospel (Gal 1.6–9) and John called on the readers of his epistles to give no sanctuary to false prophets (1 John 4.1–3; 2 John 9.11). The Lord Himself warned the five morally—and spiritually—troubled churches of Asia to repent (Rev 2–3). Other passages indicate that churches and individual saints were not to endure corrupt and faithless Christians among them (Rom 16.17; 1 Tim 1.3–4; 6.3–5; Tit 1.9–13; 3.9–11).

From this we judge that the Lord intends His people to, as best they can, keep themselves and the churches of which they are a part free from corrupting impurities. Otherwise, how can we be "the salt of the earth" and "the light of the world," bringing glory to our Father through our good lives (Matt 5.13–16)? And how can we be seen as "lights in the world, holding forth the word of life" (Phil 2.15–16)?

And yet as much as we would wish to keep the churches of the saints free of any who are not fully committed to Christ, it is a goal that human limitations will not allow us to fully achieve. As Paul observed to Timothy, "Some men's sins are clearly evident, preceding them to judgment, but those of some men follow later" (1 Tim 5.24). The same limitations that make it impossible for us to bring final judgment against others make it equally impossible for us to rid the church absolutely of all its pretenders. We can and should act upon that sinfulness of attitude and conduct that is open but, unlike God, we are not omniscient. Men can hide their shame from our eyes. Therefore, the final cleansing of the church is left for the One who knows all things. In speaking of ultimate judgment, Paul warns that we should "… judge nothing before the time, until the Lord comes, who will both bring to light the hidden things of darkness and reveal the counsels of the hearts. Then each one's praise will come from God" (1 Cor 4.5). The perfect purity of the kingdom is God's, not ours, to accomplish.

Learning to Plant with Patience

> And He said, "The kingdom of God is as if a man should scatter seed on the ground, and should sleep by night and rise by day, and the seed should sprout and grow, he himself does not know how. For the earth yields crops by itself: first the blade, then the head, after that the full grain in the head. But when the grain ripens, immediately he puts it in the sickle because the harvest has come." (Mark 4.26–27)

There is an expression in the Psalms characteristic especially of David that says, "Wait on the Lord." "Wait on the Lord; be of good courage, and He will strengthen your heart…" (27.14). This is the message of the parable of the *Growing Seed*, a parable which Mark alone gives us. And because He places it among the parables of the kingdom which we have been studying, those first which Jesus used in a teaching session beside the Sea of Galilee, we add it here to the seven which Matthew records (ch 13). It was likely among those parables which Jesus spoke only to His disciples (Matt 13.36; Mark 4.10), and therefore has particular, if not exclusive, application to them.

The parable seems as simple and straightforward as to need no special interpretation, and Jesus gives none, but it has been the occasion of considerable disagreement. Who is the sower? Jesus, or His disciples? When is the harvest? Within time or at its end? What process is illustrated? The spiritual growth of the individual disciple or the progress of the kingdom as a whole? A. B. Bruce complained that "Few of Our Lord's parables have been more unsatisfactorily expounded," but some of his own speculations are hardly better than those he criticizes in Trench and others.

Perhaps the problem arises from too much speculation about matters which are not the emphasis of Jesus' story. The focus of the parable is not on the sower or the field but upon the orderly process by which a planted seed of grain germinates and develops to maturity by a power resident in itself. There are two busy seasons in the growing of crops—seed time and harvest time. In between are weeks and months of patient waiting for a process which is beyond human power to work its' wonders. Meanwhile, the farmer goes about other tasks, busy in the usual cycle of working and sleeping. The farmer's behavior does not reflect a passive unconcern, but the simple recognition that what happens now is the work of the seed, not the sower. There are times when the only sensible thing to do is to wait, and to trust.

The focus of the parable of the *Sower* was on the soil—the influence of the heart on what happens to the planted gospel seed. In the parable of the *Growing Seed*, the focus narrows to the good soil, the good heart, and the process by which the gospel achieves its purpose in a receptive mind. The parable appears to be spoken primarily to those who are sowing the kingdom seed and is an exhortation to patient trust. When the Lord's disciples have diligently scattered abroad the gospel, they need to trust the results to the awesome transforming power of God that is resident in the message (Rom 1.16); and the absence of immediate results should never deter them from continued enthusiastic preaching of Christ on every occasion and in every place.

There is work for us to do, but the "exceeding greatness of the power is of God and not of ourselves" (2 Cor 4.7). So, to God be the glory! As God once reminded Moses, it does not so much matter who we are as who He is (Exod 2.10–14). For this reason it makes no difference if the gospel seed is planted by some Ph.D. of spiritual agriculture or a newly converted saint, the seed will germinate and grow *of itself*! As the apostle Paul once observed to some Christians impressed with preachers and their skills: "Who then is Paul and who is Apollos, but ministers through whom you believed, *as the Lord gave to each one*? I planted, Apollos watered, but God gave the increase" (1 Cor 3.5–6).

But this is just not a problem of those who think too pridefully of human skills, but of those humble souls who anxiously fret about their own inadequacies as teachers. Here again it needs to be asserted that what happens to the planted seed does not hinge on our skills or the lack of them but upon the word of God itself. We don't have to be fine tuning things all the time, always trying to pick up a stitch we think we may have missed. We need simply to say to others what Jesus has said, and that powerful eternal word will be working while we are sleeping!

An Incredible Story

The parables of Jesus arose late in His public preaching. His beginning parables, the great series on the kingdom, were taught beside the Sea of Galilee near the end of His second teaching year. The rest came in the last year of His life when He was much pressed with the need to prepare the Twelve for the events and duties which were soon to fall upon them. This is especially apparent in the parable of the *Unmerciful Servant* (Matt 18.21–35). It seems to be an integral part of a continuing conversation that began in Capernaum (compare Mark 9.33–37 with Matt 18.15).

This powerful story, so unbelievable in some of its particulars, is a fitting climax to a discussion begun with another carnal argument of the disciples over who would be greatest in the kingdom. Jesus has attempted again to warn the disciples about His coming suffering and death (Matt 17.22–23), but their continuing fascination with "greatness" revealed that they understood nothing and were still in the grip of a self-seeking pride. From this spiritual cancer arises a heedlessness and harshness toward one's "inferiors" which is compounded by a disposition never to fully admit one's own wrongs.

Jesus does not deal gently with the Twelve. Passing over them entirely, He chooses at random a little child whose humble simplicity He says exemplifies the greatness they must find if they are ever to be fit for the kingdom of heaven. He then issues a very stern warning that anyone whose vain ambitions should cause one of His disciples to stumble would be better off dead and speaks ominously of "the eternal fire" (Matt 18.6–8). To this is added instruction on the need to deal redemptively with those who sin against us, being quick to seek reconciliation through repentance and forgiveness (Matt 18.15–17). The thrust of Jesus' words was: be merciful, unresentful, easily entreated, willing to forgive.

Peter's response to all this shows that he has heard what Jesus was saying but totally missed the point. His answer is statistical, not spiritual. "Lord, how often shall my brother sin against me, and I forgive him? Up to seven times?" There is probably little doubt that Peter felt his proposal to be remarkably generous. Rabbinical tradition said three times (based erroneously on Job 33.29–30 and Amos 1.3–2.6), but sometimes never made that. The Talmud tells the story of a Rabbi who would not forgive a very small slight to his dignity though asked by the offender thirteen years in succession and that on the Day of Atonement!

Jesus' answer to Peter removes all questions of how many. "Seventy times seven" simply stands for infinity. Mercy is a quality, not a quantity. Peter's approach suggests that forgiveness is the temporary forfeiture of a right which might at some point be reclaimed. Jesus wants him to understand that no such right exists and tells the story of a merciless servant to dramatize His point.

The story which contains three scenes is full of some incredible things. First there is the incredible sum which the servant of the king has stolen or squandered—10,000 talents! That was a sum 50 times larger than the annual taxes which Herod Antipas collected from Galilee and Perea (200 talents) and more than 10 times the annual revenue of the whole of Palestine (Josephus, *Antiquities*, XVII, xi, 4). How would even a royal servant get his hands on, much less manage to steal or lose, a sum like that?!

But that is only the first remarkable detail in this story. He didn't come to the king, he was "brought," and that's not surprising, but the kind of appeal he makes is. This servant who has lost a king's ransom and is not remotely likely to be trusted again with a dime pleads for more time so that he can repay all of it! With a little time he will take care of everything. About as much chance of that as subzero temperatures in Hawaii. What a ridiculously impossible suggestion. And yet he made it. It had to be desperation or sheer bravado.

Yet that is not as surprising as the king's response. The king forgave him! A most unlikely treatment from an oriental ruler. Even kings would suffer from a loss like this, and suffer markedly.

And though there was utterly no hope of recovering the money, the man has made a fool of him in a way that no other person should be tempted to repeat. An example would be needed to deter that, and a very severe one. And yet, inexplicably, he forgave this scoundrel everything. What extraordinary grace!

An Incredible Story (2)

As we have said, the parable of the *Unmerciful Servant* (Matt 18.21–35) is an incredible story. The enormous debt the royal servant amassed is staggering, the kind of appeal he makes for release beggars credulity, and the king's response—he forgives this unmitigated scoundrel everything!—is astonishing. And yet the surprises do not end there. There is yet one final turn that caps the climax.

The second scene of the story opens with the wonderfully forgiven servant leaving the presence of the king. He has been delivered from a fate worse than death. Yet, with the ink hardly dry on his own pardon for millions, this mindless ingrate catches sight of a "fellow servant" who owes him a few dollars and nearly throttles the poor fellow while roughly demanding full and immediate payment! This is truly incredible, that a man so forgiven could be so unforgiving. It does not even seem to touch him that his debtor appeals for mercy from the same posture and in the very words he himself has so recently used. It is also ironic that while his own appeal for time to pay was ridiculous, there was a real chance this man could have paid his debt.

We are made to wonder what was going on in the mind of the forgiven servant. Was he congratulating himself on how clever he had been to escape certain disaster? Did he think the king a fool for falling for his line and vow that he would never be caught in such sentimental nonsense? Or is it conceivable that he was so dull as to see no connection between his own situation and that of his fellow? Jesus does not say.

The scene changes for the last time. Some of the king's servants who have witnessed the whole process are so dismayed by it that they report it to their master. The king, now deeply angry where he has been graciously forgiving, recalls the offending servant. Now he declares him to be "wicked," not for his original malfeasance, but because, having received such incredible mercy, he had none to give. He is forthwith turned over to men who will painfully see that he pays for every dime! The unmerciful servant had decided that he wanted to play justice rather than mercy and his lord abundantly accommodates him.

Jesus makes the point of His story exceedingly clear. "So My Heavenly Father will also do to you if each of you, from his heart, does not forgive his brother his trespasses" (Matt 18.35). And this is no obscure lesson. Jesus frequently speaks to it in the Sermon on the Mount: "Blessed are the merciful, for they shall obtain mercy" (Matt 5.7). "And forgive us our debts as we forgive our debtors" (Matt 6.12). "Judge not that you be not judged. For with what judgment you judge you will be judged; and with the measure you use it shall be measured back to you" (Matt 7.1–2). And nearer the time of our parable the Lord warns His disciples, "Take heed to yourselves. If your brother sins against you, rebuke him; and if he repents, forgive him. And if he sins against you seven times in a day, and seven times in a day returns to you saying, 'I repent,' you shall forgive him" (Luke 17.3–4).

The enormity of our sins against God is aptly illustrated by the servant's impossibly large debt to the king. And the small debt owed to him by his fellow servant speaks well of how tiny by comparison are the injuries others may inflict on us. Shakespeare's Macbeth, speaking of his own deep guilt, says that the whole ocean would not suffice to wash the blood from his hands, but would in fact dye the whole sea red. It becomes inconceivable then that those forgiven so much could refuse to forgive so little. And yet how many Christians rise from the Lord's Supper to go out and live with merciless hardness in daily life?

The problem is that too many of us want to live with God under grace, but with men, under law. With our Father we want mercy but with others we want justice. We can't have it both ways, and when we try we are truly "wicked." It is bad enough for us to have sinned against God's righteous law, but how much more grievous must it be for us to treat His gracious mercy with contempt? "Of how much worse punishment, do you suppose, will he be thought worthy who has trampled the Son of God underfoot, counted the blood of the covenant by which he is sanctified a common thing, and insulted the Spirit of grace?" (Heb 10.29) And when those of us who have received such mercy from God refuse to show it to others, we have surely done no less. "It is a fearful thing to fall into the hands of the living God" (Heb 10.31).

A Nameless Woman We Will Never Forget

The teaching of Jesus on forgiveness has been little understood in our times. The grace of God has been widely and enthusiastically preached, but often with such irreverent presumption that its cost to God and its demand from us, both of a deep sense of the need for pardon and a profound gratitude for it, are little treated. Jesus addresses this critical matter in the parable of *The Two Debtors* (Luke 7.36–50).

In the parable of *The Unmerciful Servant* Jesus illustrates how God's incredible mercy toward us should transform our attitude toward others. In the parable of *The Two Debtors* He unlocks the secret of those who love God in a surpassing way and, in so doing, reveals the reason why some men and women, in great need of mercy themselves, are so callous, judgmental, and unforgiving.

The story which gives rise to this parable is a very powerful one, so much so that the parable rests in its shadow, a simple little illustration which serves to explain the moving scene which has just been played out. We do not know with exactness the time or place of the teaching of the parable of *The Two Debtors*, but it must have been in one of the cities of Galilee and likely in the Lord's second year of public teaching. Luke places it at a time in his narrative which would make it the earliest of Jesus' parables, but it cannot be known for sure if it actually occurred then or was inserted to illustrate why Jesus, as His detractors loved to repeat, had a reputation as the friend of sinners. The fact that the Lord is still getting dinner invitations from Pharisees and the generally quiet atmosphere of this one would suggest a time before the bitter confrontations of the final year when His last dinner date with a Pharisee exploded in a powerful denunciation of their hypocrisy (Luke 11.37–44).

Jesus, as open to the high as to the lowly, has answered the dinner invitation of a Pharisee named Simon. Simon's motives are difficult to gauge. Perhaps it was curiosity about a popular religious teacher or the desire to parade a "celebrity" at his dinner table. He knows that Jesus is seen by many as a prophet, but his manner with him seems more patronizingly polite than thoughtful and respectful.

Into this otherwise ordinary setting comes suddenly a woman of notorious reputation who falls at Jesus' extended feet and without a word covers them with ardent kisses. The Lord, also unspeaking, quietly continues His meal, neither recoiling from her touch nor reproving her forwardness. Simon, too, is speechless, too taken aback for words, but not for some very indicting thoughts against the woman and against Jesus. "If Jesus does not know what kind of woman this is," he reasons, "He cannot be a prophet, and if He knows and does not reject her He cannot be truly good." For Simon, just the touch of such a woman was defiling (v 39).

Such behavior on the part of a woman of ill-fame at the home of a prominent Pharisee was bound to cause a sensation. She was, first of all, not ordinary, and secondly she did not observe from the periphery as uninvited strangers were evidently permitted by custom to do in the ancient world, but came directly up to Jesus. Given her reputation and Simon's mindset, it is not surprising that He suspected her fervent kisses to be of a different sort than they were. He drew a quick conclusion that was as untrue as it was "logical," and in his haste was grievously unfair to both the woman and Jesus.

She came to Him. The background of this "sinful" woman is shrouded in silence. There is not the slightest evidence that she was either Mary of Bethany (an honorable woman of a well-respected household) or Mary Magdalene (from whom Jesus cast out seven demons, never a sign of wickedness). We can only speculate that she had, like thousands of others, heard the gracious invitation of Jesus for burdened sinners to come to Him for rest, and, believing, had come to the Lord in penitence and joyful gratitude (v 50). The woman came to Jesus, not impulsively, but resolutely, and prepared her heart so completely fixed on the Son of God that she was wholly unconscious of how her behavior was affecting others.

She wept. The only thing unplanned in this sinful woman's actions was the sudden flood of tears that her broken but thankful heart sent cascading down upon Jesus' feet. Hastily she wipes away the offending drops with her released tresses, and now drawn close, kisses His feet in gratitude and homage. It is likely that only after composing herself does she pour out upon Him the alabaster cruse of aromatic oil which she had brought to honor Him.

Short of the crucifixion, there is not a more moving scene in the Bible, and because of it, Jesus has given us the parable of *The Two Debtors*.

"I Have Something to Say to You"

Jesus' parable of the *Two Debtors* (Luke 7.36–50) is calculated to help a profoundly critical Pharisee to see himself in contrast to the notorious woman who has just scandalized him by anointing the feet of Jesus. The Lord was the only one in the banquet room not staring in stunned silence at the sinful woman kneeling penitently at His feet. His concern was with His host who had been looking on the woman with utter disgust and upon Jesus with disdain. Jesus broke the silence by speaking, not with the woman but with him, "Simon, I have something to say to you." The moment is electric.

The Pharisee's harsh, judgmental self-righteousness deserves a severe rebuke. He has put the worst possible interpretation on the woman's behavior because it does not enter his mind that sinful people could change, nor does he seem to have any longing for it. But the rebuke does not come. Instead, Jesus calmly tells a story of two debtors obligated to the same lender. One owed the equivalent of nearly two years' wages (500 denarii) and the other that of about two months' (50 denarii) but because neither was able to pay, the creditor forgave them both.

Jesus focuses His story by asking Simon which of the two debtors he thinks would love his gracious benefactor more. "He, I suppose, to whom he forgave the most," he answers off-handedly (if not condescendingly), as if he sees no point in the parable but is willing to go along for the ride. But Simon is already caught as Jesus tells him that his answer is correct.

The Lord applies the parable by asking Simon, "Do you see this woman?" (He has been looking at nothing else, but he has not *seen* her.) Jesus notes that while Simon had not even provided him the ordinary amenities due a guest—a welcoming kiss, water with which to wash His feet, oil to anoint His head, the offending woman had kissed his feet repeatedly while she anointed them with fragrant oil, washed them with her tears, and wiped them with her hair. Then He draws His gracious noose more tightly as He explains the reason for her lavish, loving behavior as contrasted with Simon's thoughtless indifference. She loved much because she had much for which to be forgiven—her sins were many. "But to whom little is forgiven, the same loves little." Jesus did not need to be more specific. By His own words Simon had already judged himself.

Simon's problem was not that with few sins to his credit he was denied a true sense of gratitude for being forgiven. It was his perception of his sins as few that was destroying him. A man who conceives himself as a moral and spiritual paragon will have great difficulty bearing gently with those whom he sees as grievous moral failures. And he will have equal difficulty in feeling any sense of gratitude toward God. In truth, Simon's sins were many, but he was blind both to them and to God's grace.

In a similar way, the woman's joyous and prodigal appreciation did not come from having sinned more than all others but from having understood the true seriousness of her own moral failure. Her sins had been socially reprehensible, but Saul of Tarsus, whose life had been spent studying and practicing the law of God, also saw himself as "the chief of sinners" and spent the rest of his days celebrating and proclaiming the wonders of God's grace (1 Tim 1.12–17; Eph 3.8–9). He, too, in a figure fell at the feet of Jesus, wept out his gratitude, and poured out his life like anointing oil.

I am not so sure that in this parable Jesus intends to say that the wrongs of human beings can be put on a quantifiable scale of seriousness. Perhaps one man's sins can be more grievous than another's. But whatever the case, as the parable makes clear; none of us can pay our debt. We are all hopelessly entangled in transgression and the result of our sins, few or many, will be essential death (Rom 3.23; 6.23). The person who lives to do his own will is a rebel against God, however urbanely it may be expressed. Jesus closes His conversation with Simon by telling him plainly that the many sins of the woman who has given him such offense are forgiven and then, turning to the woman herself, He says, "Your sins are forgiven. ...Your faith has saved you; go in peace." The "scarlet woman" leaves Jesus forgiven, love-filled, and joyful. So far as we know, Simon "the righteous" ends his time with the Son of God unforgiven, unmerciful, and unchanged. Perhaps all he got for his experience was another reason to reject Jesus. A man who claims to forgive sin... who can believe a word he says?

Learning to Care Enough

Jesus' story of the *Good Samaritan* (Luke 10.25–37) has in it all the compelling ingredients of modern journalism: greed, crime, violence, suffering, racial hatred, social unconcern, love, and compassion. What, after all, is new? The gospel speaks well to modern man.

This story was told by Jesus because some time during the fall of the year before He died, a lawyer (expert in Jewish law) questioned Him about the way to gain eternal life. He was not asking for information, but checking to see if the Lord was up to speed on the law. We are bound to wonder about his motives. Was he just trying to be clever and expose this "uneducated" rabbi? Was he chafing under the severe attacks Jesus had leveled against the hypocrisy and ignorance of men of his class? Or was it an honest effort to test the Lord's claims? For such men the law was usually more a subject for disputation than a guide to life. He knew well what it said and answered quickly when Jesus turned the question back over to the "expert"—"Love God with all your heart, soul, strength, and mind, and your neighbor as yourself," he said. Just as quickly, Jesus put the matter where it needed to be: "You know the truth, but life comes by living it."

The lawyer, left looking a bit foolish for asking a question with so obvious an answer, tries to rescue himself from losing an argument by raising another problem. "That's all well and good," he seems to say, "but how do I know who my neighbor is?" Jewish scribes were known to make very careful distinctions between "neighbors" and "strangers." Jesus answers this question, not with another question or an exemplary statement, but with a penetrating story.

The setting was a familiar one—the road from Jerusalem down to Jericho, a steep descent which in 22 miles drops 3,500 feet through a rocky desolation rent by hundreds of rugged ravines. Except for a modern highway, the scene remains just as desolate today. In Jesus' time, it was a notorious hangout for thieves and brigands.

The lesson is carried in the interplay of the characters Jesus chose to meet "by chance" on that desolate stretch. There is first the unfortunate victim, "a certain man" who has been seriously wounded, stripped of his clothing, and left half-dead in the desert by thieves. Without help, he was destined to die alone in this arid waste. He could have been any man, high or low, rich or poor. We think of him as a Jew, but that is not stated or even implied.

The Thieves

The men who robbed him, with one thing only in mind, were as uncaring as a pack of snarling wolves. They used him like a paper towel and threw him away when he had no further use. We are not likely to be so brutal, but we use people nonetheless, even in religious settings. We use them to feed our egos or to satisfy our own selfish purposes, and then when they no longer serve us, push them aside. It is a sophisticated kind of cruelty.

The Priest and Levite

Upon this pathetic scene first appear a priest and a Levite; men noted above all others for their religious piety. Their presence on this road would not have been unusual since these special servants of God had to come twice a year to serve a week in the Temple (1 Chron 24) and would either have to travel from Jericho, a city of priests, or from Galilee through Jericho so as to avoid Samaria. From such men whose task it was to bless and serve their people, there was every reason to expect compassion. There was none. They passed by "on the other side." But the tragedy is that Jesus is not pointing in this to the unusual, but to the usual: as usual as thieves on the road to Jericho was this compassionless "piety" that is concerned for the suffering but not enough to overcome the fear or the inconvenience. They no doubt had many good reasons for not stopping—more important things to do, can't risk defilement for temple service, no good getting two men robbed instead of one; you can't help all these people. Or perhaps as some cynical humorist once observed, they could see that the man had been robbed already! No doubt they expressed their outrage at all this violence as they passed cautiously by.

This part of the story might have been directed at the lawyer with his cold, didactic religiosity, but who among us has not played it safe when suddenly confronted by the physical or spiritual misery of others? We are put off by the risk to ourselves or the inconvenience to our schedule or the pain of shared suffering or the simple demand of time and money. We, too, can talk glibly about loving others, but all too often it has no meaning.

Welcome to the Neighborhood

No love had been lost between the Jews and Samaritans since the days of the Return when Samaritan leaders intrigued continually to prevent the rebuilding of Jerusalem. In Jesus' day, the relationship was still bitter. Jews had no dealings with Samaritans (John 4.9) and used the term as an ultimate expression of abuse (John 8.18). The villages of Samaria in turn were not hospitable to Jews traveling through the region to Jerusalem (Luke 9.51–55). During the reign of Claudius Caesar, some Samaritans massacred a group of Jewish pilgrims in the northern border village of Ginae (*Antiquities*, XX, xi, 1).

This explains why Jesus used a Samaritan to illustrate the meaning of neighbor love. It spoke directly to Jewish prejudice. In the Lord's story, this half-breed outcast was the only one with sufficient compassion to stop and help a desperately wounded man (Luke 10.25–37). More than merely touched by the tragedy of the man, the Samaritan acted. He gently tended his wounds and transported him to the nearest inn where he made provision for his complete care. This was no grand but short-lived gesture. His concern and involvement were total.

By the time Jesus had finished telling the story of the man robbed and beaten by thieves and had concluded it by asking, "Who proved neighbor to him that fell among the robbers?" The lawyer who had begun this conversation was likely wishing he had never opened his mouth. He had evidently raised the question about what one had to do to inherit eternal life merely for argument's sake, but Jesus had compelled him to answer his own question. He had asked the question about who his neighbor was only to rescue himself from embarrassment, but now he must answer again. Unwilling even to identify the Samaritan, the lawyer says, "He that showed mercy on him." Whereupon Jesus moves everything from theory to practice. "Go, and do likewise," He said.

Luke does not record the impact of all this upon the lawyer. One thing is sure. He had learned a great deal about the size of his neighborhood. It was as wide as the world, and his neighbor was anyone who needed his help.

There were other lessons too. The priest and Levite were wrong to put sacrifice ahead of goodness. Loving God does not make one merciless toward men. Jesus had once made this point from the words of Hosea: "For I desire goodness and not sacrifice; and the knowledge of God more than burnt offerings" (6.6; Matt 9.13). John would later put it in plain terms. "If a man say I love God, and hate his brother, he is a liar; for he that does not love his brother whom he has seen, cannot love God whom he has not seen" (1 John 4.20). Even an appointment to worship God cannot be used to justify turning one's back on the suffering. If we find ourselves in our passion for God abandoning all consideration of others, we can be assured that we are under the control of a misbegotten passion. Some are of the tragically mistaken persuasion that any abuse of others is justified when one is trying to maintain the truth of God.

A further lesson is found in the truth that the Samaritan was not responding to some nobility in the unfortunate stranger. He had no idea of the man's moral character. Neighbor love is not a response to the goodness in others, but to their need. Had the man fallen into such desperate straits by his own carelessness it would have changed nothing. He could have been a Jew who had himself treated Samaritans with contempt or simply by his race stirred memories of the injustices of others. It is not easy to forget old injuries and they get readily generalized to whole populations. But true neighbor love moves only out of concern for what in similar circumstances one would want for himself. It is not a response to the thoughtfulness of others, but a pure act of love toward those who may never have befriended us in any way.

Finally, there is this fundamental, over-arching lesson. When asked about how to obtain eternal life, Jesus sent the lawyer right back to the Scripture. In our search for answers to transcendent questions we are unduly disposed to think the Bible too difficult to yield clear answers. The Lord knows better. The word of God is clear enough for those who want to do His will. Were we today to have opportunity to stand in the very presence of the Son of God and raise our difficult questions with Him, He would say to us what He said to that Jewish lawyer, "What is written in the word of God? What is your reading of it?" The answers are there if only we have the courage to receive and apply them.

With Jesus in the School of Prayer

Jesus' stories of the *Friend at Midnight* (Luke 11.1–13) and the *Importunate Widow* (Luke 18.1–8) are so strikingly similar in purpose that they can be considered twin parables. Luke's chronology indicates they were not spoken together, but both are part of a long section of his Gospel which is set against the background of a journey to Jerusalem (9.51–19.27). Jesus' subject in these two parables is prayer and there is much in them we all need to learn.

Parable of the Friend at Midnight (Luke 11.1–13)
The parable of the *Friend at Midnight* was occasioned by the request of one of Jesus' disciples who, stirred by the earnest supplications of his Master, entreated Him to teach them to pray.

The select group of Jesus' disciples who lived daily with Him and heard Him teach so often were no doubt astonished like others at the wisdom and grace with which He spoke (Matt 7.28–29; John 7.45–46). As far as we know, not one of them ever asked Jesus to teach them how to preach, even though preaching was to be their mission. They must have realized that the secret of the life of Jesus resided not so much in His preaching skill as in His relationship with His Father. They had seen something special in watching Him pray, and perhaps wanted to share in the intimacy, the absolute confidence in God which they had observed in Him. They recognized, too, that if they did not learn to pray it would not be just a disadvantage but a disaster. If Jesus, who was God in the flesh, needed to pray often and at times at great length in order to do His Father's will (Luke records eight occasions), how much more the mere human beings who follow Him. Any Christian who is not wise and diligent in prayer is on the road to spiritual bankruptcy.

Jesus responds to the disciple's request by repeating the model prayer that He had taught in the Sermon on the Mount (Luke 11.2–4; Matt 6.9–13). The Lord was not saying by this that the secret of His prayer filled life was the correct repeating of some ritual. The model prayer rather stresses the priorities of the spiritual life—that the true life of prayer rests on relationship ("Our Father") and an overarching concern that above all other things God should be glorified and His will done. All the rest of our petitions and our life must serve that one supreme end.

True prayer is at last an earnest search for the will of God. Warren Wiersbe quotes Robert Law as saying, "Prayer is a mighty instrument, not for getting man's will done in heaven, but for getting God's will done on earth."

To the model prayer Jesus adds the parable of the *Friend at Midnight*. To understand this story it is important to know that hospitality was a significant social obligation in the Middle East, and that the ordinary house of the times had one large room, the front two-thirds with a packed earth, straw-strewn floor where animals were often housed at night, and in the back a small raised platform where the family ate and slept.

Jesus suggests that there were none of His hearers who, faced with unexpected guests at midnight, could not by sheer doggedness get some needed food from an already sleeping neighbor. It must have been a familiar experience in first-century Palestine. You can imagine the scene. A friend shows up at your door in the middle of the night and the bread baked for the preceding day has already been eaten. What to do? You go to your friend's house where the door, open wide during the day, has already been shut and bolted and he and his family are fast asleep. You knock until your friend is roused out of a sound slumber and ask him kindly for the loan of some bread. He responds in surly astonishment, "What are you doing knocking on my door at this hour of the night and asking for bread of all things? Go away and leave me alone before you wake up the whole house." You knock again. The children who took so long to settle down are now awake and asking questions: "Is it morning? Can we get up?" You keep on knocking. Now even the neighbors are getting up to see what the ruckus is about. Desperate, your friend finally gets up and jerks open the door to tell you to take all the bread you want but to please let him and his family get some sleep. Everyone knows, Jesus concludes His story, that even when friendship means nothing, "persistence" pays off (v 8). The Greek word translated *persistence* actually means *shamelessness*.

With this humorous illustration from the workaday world (Did Jesus have a twinkle in His eye as He told it?), Jesus sets the stage to teach us some vital lessons about prayer. *(To be continued)*

Unyielding Prayer

The parable of the *Importunate Widow* (Luke 18.18) is a virtual twin to the parable of the *Friend at Midnight* though Jesus taught it months later (sometime during the winter before He died). Both parables teach the same lesson, "that man ought always to pray and not lose heart" (Luke 18.1).

Jesus' story is of a widow without resource or advocate who seeks justice from a certain Judge against her "adversary." Was he trying to rob her of the land by which she lived, or to defraud her of some meager but vital inheritance from her deceased husband? The Lord does not say, but her case was being stymied by the unyielding corruption of the magistrate who, devoid by his own admission of either conscience or compassion, was moved only by self interest.

Such judges must have been common in ancient Israel because the prophets are filled with denunciations of their injustices. "Your princes are rebellious and companions of thieves; everyone loves bribes, and follows after rewards; they do not judge the fatherless, neither does the cause of the widow come to them" (Isa 1.23; see also Jer 5.28; Ezek 22.7; Mal 3.5). The Talmud accuses some village judges of ignorance, arbitrariness, and covetousness so great that they would pervert justice for a dish of meat.

It was to just such a judge, not only hard but profoundly sorry, that this defenseless widow in her desperation came (the imperfect tense of the Greek verb indicates a continual coming). There would be only three ways to move such a judge—bribery, intimidation, or supplication. Without money or power, she was left to plead with the persistence of despair (Buttrick). It was a situation absolutely overwhelmed with hopelessness.

Yet in this woman, this "Tugboat Annie," the calloused magistrate met his match. He may have been assaulted by dogged persistence before, but none to equal this woman's endless and unyielding appeals. She met him every time he turned around and hit him in the only place he could be hit—his selfish concern for his own comfort. He granted her justice, not because he was just or even compassionate, but because he realized that he would never know a moment's peace until he did.

So both the man with an unexpected guest and the widow fighting for her rights illustrate the power of a shameless persistence even against an uncaring neighbor and an unjust judge. But how are we to apply these parables to the children of God praying to their Father?

The attitude of the neighbor or the judge surely does not represent the attitude of God toward His children, even though it can sometimes appear to the anguished and struggling Christian that the Lord is unheeding. What these parables argue is that if persistent appeals can move the uncaring, how much more the caring of God. A. B. Bruce sees these two parables as Jesus' effort to reconcile the often puzzling trials of life with the truth of God's loving providence for His people.

We must also struggle with the fact that in both parables persistence in prayer is said to bring the desired answer. Immediately upon His telling of the parable of the *Friend at Midnight*, Jesus says plainly: "For everyone who asks receives, and he who seeks finds, and to him who knocks it will be opened" (Luke 11.10). It is not a matter of our continual pleading obtaining from God anything we might wish (2 Cor 12.8–9). The Lord will not give His children a stone instead of bread, no matter how steadfastly they beseech Him. And there are no clever formulas which put Him in our power. Jesus has already warned about the "vain repetitions" of the heathen who "think they will be heard for their many words" (Matt 6.7). But whatever the subject of these petitions might be, the Lord is clearly assuring us that an unfailing longing, expressed in constant entreaties, will bring from God the desired result.

Perhaps the key that unlocks all this is Jesus' concluding statement in His conversation with the disciples about prayer: "If you then, being evil, know how to give good gifts to your children, how much more will your heavenly Father give the Holy Spirit to those who ask Him" (Luke 11.13). The "good gifts" of God do not include all we might ask for, however often, but only that which serves our salvation in the kingdom of God (the work of the Holy Spirit). Anything that does not serve God's eternal purpose for us will be withheld. This then is our assurance: all that seek salvation in Christ will find it; all that ask for the "true bread" will receive it; all that knock for entrance into Heaven's kingdom will find the door open. But these parables also stress that the seeking must not be casual, the asking half-hearted, and the knocking indifferent. God cannot give Himself to those who do not seek Him earnestly and with a whole heart (Matt 6.33). Unyielding prayer rises from an unyielding faith.

A Fool and His Money

> When one from the crowd said to Him, "Teacher, tell my brother to divide the inheritance with me." But He said to him, "Man, who made Me a judge or an arbitrator over you?" And He said to them, "Take heed and beware of covetousness, for one's life does not consist in the abundance of the things he possesses." (Luke 12.13–15)

Somewhere, most likely in Judea, in the fall of the year before He died, Jesus was surrounded by an excited multitude of so many thousands that they were trampling one another (Luke 12.1). With a sense of urgency He seeks to prepare His disciples for the then unimaginable dark days when their only defense against a brutal persecution would be to fear God alone and trust Him for all things.

This intense moment, filled with the Lord's earnest exhortations about heavenly things, was suddenly interrupted by a request that fairly jarred the air into which it intruded. Some man in the crowd was asking Jesus to intervene in a dispute over an inheritance. One can imagine that the silence hung very heavy for a time. When the Lord answered, it was a strong rebuke.

The questioner had evidently heard nothing the Lord was saying. His heart was altogether too preoccupied with money to have any interest in eternal things. What he wanted was the services of this influential teacher in fulfilling his material agenda. His wrong was not in seeking what was not rightfully his (he is not charged with unrighteousness), nor in wanting the help of some wise and godly man to adjudicate a family dispute (1 Cor 6.5). His problem lay in an obsession with things so great that he could stand and listen to the transcendent words of the Son of God and see in Him nothing more than a tool for his own ambitions. He wanted to "use" Jesus not to follow Him. He saw Him not as the Savior of men, but as a petty judge.

The Lord did not accommodate him, and He will not accommodate us. Too many of us want Jesus to solve our problems but not to change our hearts. He was no more interested in the mundane job this man had in mind for Him than He was in being the king of bread to some carnal Galileans (John 6.15). He had come to save lost men from eternal destruction (Luke 19.10) and had no intention of helping this man any further down the road to ruin.

The man who made this untoward request was to be pitied. He thought his troubles would be over if he could just get his inheritance. He was convinced the problem was his brother's greed when it was his own love of things that was killing him. But Jesus warned him, and the surrounding multitude, that he was a victim of that perverse philosophy (covetousness) which says that a man's life consists "in the abundance of the things he possesses." In short, what you have is what you are. This misbegotten idea is pernicious, for the more one seeks enlargement by the accumulation of goods, the more the soul is starved and contracted—the greater the wealth, the larger the spiritual void.

The word Jesus uses for "life" here is *zoe*, essential life, rather than *bios*, livelihood (Mark 12.44). We live in a material world and have material needs, the lack of which can threaten our physical lives but they cannot deny nor provide true life (Luke 12.4–5). Jesus never condemned wealth and from His humble circumstance never envied it either, but He warned of its seductive temptations (Luke 18.21–25; 16.13). He warned about trusting it as the essence of life. That, He said, will kill you. Paul echoes His master in strong terms: "But those who desire to be rich fall into temptation and a snare, and into many foolish and harmful lusts which drown men in destruction and perdition. For the love of money is the root of all kinds of evil…" (1 Tim 6.9–10). Covetousness is that spiritual disease which causes a man to be more concerned about time than eternity and anxiety for this life has choked out all interest in the life to come.

As George Buttrick has observed, this is revolutionary teaching, and even while we faithfully repeat the Lord's warning we do not believe it very deeply. We still find identity and meaning in our material holdings and feel stripped of consequence when they are diminished. Too many of us are like this sad man who was found in the very presence of Jesus without a clue as to what life was about. We spend our days in church assemblies and learn only to serve ourselves. The man in our text needed, as we often do, to see himself for the blind dupe he was. So the Lord held up the mirror to him in His parable of the *Rich Fool* (Luke 12.16–21).

Rich Toward God

> Then He spoke a parable to them saying: "The ground of a certain rich man yielded plentifully. And he thought within himself, saying, 'What shall I do, since I have no room to store my crops?' So he said, 'I will pull down my barns and build greater, and there will I store all my crops and goods. And I will say to my soul, "Soul, you have many goods laid up for many years; take your ease; eat, drink, and be merry."' But God said to him, 'Fool! This night your soul will be required of you; then whose will those things be which you have provided?' So is he who lays up treasure for himself, and is not rich toward God." (Luke 12.16–21)

So spoke Jesus to the gathered multitude who had just heard Him reprove a man who saw in Him no more than arbiter for a family money squabble. "Beware of covetousness," He said, and then told the above parable to explain why. The parable of the *Rich Fool* is a mirror to the soul.

The farmer of this parable was not some poor man who came suddenly upon wealth. He was already rich when a great harvest made his already large barns too small. There is no indication that any of the farmer's wealth was ill-gotten. For all we know he earned every bit of it by hard work and prudent management. This story is not about fraud. It's about foolishness. The farmer who had been so skillful in managing his farm turned out to be a simpleton at managing life. He made some very obvious blunders.

First of all, he made the mistake of assuming that he was the owner of his wealth. "My crops, my goods, my barns," even "my soul," he said. What arrogance! What ingratitude! As if he and he alone had achieved all this. There is not one uttered word of thanks to the great God who gives "us from heaven rain and fruitful seasons, filling our hearts with food and gladness" (Acts 14.17), not to speak of "life, breath, and all things" (Acts 17.25).

Any time we think we *own* the things we are using, it would do us good to check the abstract of the land we're on, or the houses we're in. We are all tenants here.

His second blunder was in reasoning with himself about what disposition he should make of his unexpected blessings (Luke 12.17). He should have consulted God because the world and all its fullness are His (Psa 50.12). But that never entered his mind. Nor did he think about the empty barns of poor and struggling people to whom his surplus would have meant deliverance. He thought only of himself.

His third blunder was in supposing that what he could put in a barn was all he needed. Looking over all his abundance, he said to himself, "I've got it made!" He thought these things meant assured ease, happiness, and security. One wonders what world he had been living in. As a farmer he was no stranger to blight, drought, flood, and theft. It takes uncommon blindness to imagine there's any security in things (Matt 6.19). But it requires even greater dullness to imagine that spirits formed in the image of the Eternal could ever be satisfied and fulfilled with mere matter even if it were eternal (Ecc 5.10–11; 6.7). We were made for "the living God" (Psa 42.2; Acts 17.26–28) and life issues from the heart, not the bank (Prov 4.23).

Finally, our "successful" farmer forgot about time and death. He was thinking "many years," but God said not even one more day. His wealth went one way and he went the other. There are no pockets in a shroud. Solomon frequently speaks to this truth in Ecclesiastes. "Then I hated all my labor in which I had toiled under the sun, because I must leave it to the man that will come after me. And who knows whether he will be wise or a fool?" (2.18–19). There is no greater inexcusable folly than to plan life without consideration of death and to build life on things which death will certainly take away. The evidence of our mortality and life's uncertainty is not just compelling, it is overwhelming. No truth about ourselves is as evident as the fact that we are going to die, and die at some unforeseen time. And the only thing that will survive death is a secure relationship with God. We should, therefore, pour out all our lives and treasure toward Him, heaped up, pressed down, running over.

It is said that Alexander the Great asked to be buried with his hands so placed that all could see they were empty. It is also reported that when the Emperor Charlemagne's crypt was opened he was found sitting on his throne with one now bony figure pointing to a text in an open Bible: "What will it profit a man if he gains the whole world, and loses his own soul?" (Mark 8.36). It is a very good question.

Axe at the Root:
Living on Borrowed Time

> He also spoke this parable: "A certain man had a fig tree planted in his vineyard, and he came seeking fruit on it and found none. Then he said to the keeper of his vineyard. 'Look, for three years I have come seeking fruit on this fig tree and found none. Cut it down; why does it use up the ground?' But he answered and said to him, 'Sir, let it alone this year also, until I dig around it and fertilize it. And if it bears fruit, well; but if not, after that you can cut it down.'" (Luke 13.6–9, NKJV)

This parable of Jesus speaks gravely of a last opportunity in the face of impending doom. The context tells us that it is directed at the Jewish nation. The chapter opens with Jesus' appeal for a broad scale national repentance and closes with His brokenhearted lament over the city of Jerusalem whose stubborn rejection of His love was leading them to desolation (13.34–35).

John the Baptist had first warned that time was running out for Israel. "The axe," he said," is laid at the root of the trees," and "every tree that does not bear good fruit is cut down and thrown into the fire" (Matt 3.10). And now Jesus, well into His third year of public preaching, is saying that disaster has drawn even nearer. Both called urgently for a change of heart (Matt 3.2; 4.17).

The occasion for the parable of the *Barren Fig Tree* was the report by some to Jesus of the massacre of certain Galileans "whose blood Pilate had mingled with their sacrifices" (Luke 13.1). The occupying Roman legions were a constant provocation to the restive Galileans who occasionally hurled themselves hopelessly against their oppressors only to be mercilessly crushed. We have no other record of this event, but Josephus records a sufficient number of similar incidents to make it entirely credible. Pilate had evidently caught some Galilean rebels at their devotions and dispatched them—human and animal blood flowing in grisly union.

From Jesus' response ("Do you suppose that these Galileans were worse sinners than all other Galileans because they suffered these things?") we conclude that the motive for raising this matter was not indignation but smug self-righteousness—the suggestion that men who came to such a violent end, slaughtered even in their worship, must have been truly wicked. Jesus replied that it was worse than they thought—that unless they themselves repented they would perish in similar horror. This is perhaps an allusion to the slaughter of AD 70 and certainly to a divine judgment far more dreadful. It was their own stubborn sins that needed to concern them.

The parable of the *Barren Fig Tree* is intended to give graphic force to Jesus' warning, "I tell you no, unless you repent you will all likewise perish" (Luke 13.3, 5). It is the story of a last minute reprieve for a fig tree which, though situated in a favored place in a vineyard, had for three years failed to produce a single fig. The owner, frustrated with such long barrenness, said, "Cut it down. It is a waste of good soil, time, and energy." But the vineyard keeper appeals to the owner for one more season to see if more diligent care may yet bring it to fruitfulness.

The fruitless tree symbolizes Israel, the long favored and richly blessed people of God whose faithless and treacherous ways had deeply tried the patience of God. In the Old Testament it was the vineyard itself that was an established figure for Israel (Isa 5.1–7; Psa 80.81–6). A. B. Bruce suggests that Jesus' choice of the fig tree in this parable was to show that Israel, like the fig tree in the vineyard, had no inherent right to the blessings of God. Like the fig tree they were in a favored place, not by nature or right, but by the grace of the owner and the only thing that would keep them there was fruitfulness. Privileges bring responsibilities. As Jesus would later note, even a vine has no prescriptive right in a vineyard if it is fruitless (John 15.26).

Paul makes a similar argument in Romans where, using the figure of an olive tree, he says that the Jews, who were the natural branches of the tree because the promises were spoken to them, were nevertheless broken off because of their unbelief. How much more then, he argues, did this apply to the Gentiles (wild olive branches) who were grafted in. Faithful or faithless, fruitful or fruitless; this was the primary issue which ruled over all other conditions (Rom 11.17–24).

The fate of the fig tree is left unresolved in the parable, just as the fate of Israel is. Grace and opportunity are there. It will now be determined whether Israel, having been loved and blessed by God so unheedingly for so many years (Deut 4.7–8), will at last hear the voice of God's Son who comes to pour Himself out upon them in one last grand redemptive act. Whatever the case, Israel is living on borrowed time.

This is Not a Time for Foolishness

Jesus' parable of the *Barren Fig Tree* (Luke 13.6–9) is the story of a vineyard owner whose patience is finally exhausted by the long fruitlessness of a much-favored fig tree and an interceding vineyard keeper who pleads for one more chance before the axe.

God is clearly seen in the vineyard owner and Christ in the vineyard keeper while impenitent Israel is the threatened tree. The question between the owner and keeper is not whether judgment must come upon the endlessly useless fig—but when. Though there is much of mercy and patience in this parable, the somber tones of impending retribution dominate.

While understanding that this story stood originally as a graphic warning to a privileged but rebellious people of the nearness of divine judgment, we need also to extract from it the unchanging principles which guide God's dealings with men in all ages.

The first is that we will be judged not by appearances or by mere activity but by our fruitfulness. And the fruitfulness expected will be determined by the extent of God's investment in us. It was the love He bestowed upon His beloved vineyard (Israel) and the expectation it produced that brought Him such deep dismay at its uselessness (Isa 5.1–7). In Ezekiel the Lord observes that for all the special blessings He had heaped upon His people they had turned to do worse things than the surrounding pagans (5.6). Special blessings bring special responsibilities.

This principle is unchanged in the New Testament. In connection with an appeal for God's servants to always be ready to give account, Jesus said, "For everyone to whom much is given, from him much will be required" (Luke 12.45). This should be especially meaningful to Christians upon whom God has poured out the rich treasury of His blessings in Christ (Eph 1.3).

The writer of Hebrews speaks of this when he twice asks how

in view of the swift punishment delivered to transgressors under the law we can expect to escape an even severer fate who neglect "so great a salvation" as that declared by the Lord's own mouth and sealed with His very own blood (2.2, 4; 10.28–29)? No disciple of Jesus should feel comfortable in serving Him with indifferent carelessness in the face of His profound investment in us. His expectations are just. The one who abides in Him, He said, "bears much fruit" (John 15.5).

But just what might this vital fruit be? Not a few have suggested that given Jesus' purpose in coming into this world (Luke 19.10) it must be lost souls led to salvation. There can be no question but that the disciple of Jesus must seek to save the lost, and for myself, I think there is a great likelihood that a truly fruitful disciple will during his or her lifetime lead or help to lead several others to Christ. But both Old and New Testaments make clear that it is not our ultimate responsibility to convert the unsaved but to show them the way. Ezekiel's task was to warn the wayward house of Israel (3.17–21) and "whether they hear or whether they refuse," God said, "… they will know that a prophet has been among them" (2.5). Of his own responsibility, Paul said it was planting and watering the seed while the results were left to God (1 Cor 3.6). Unfortunately, the tragedy for many of us is unsown and unwatered seed.

Then what is the fruit which we can bear without question, which is wholly within our power by God's grace to attain? It is a godly life "filled with the fruits of righteousness which are by Jesus Christ, to the glory and praise of God" (Phil 1.11). It is a character rich with the "fruit of the Spirit" (Gal 5.22–23) by the power of which we will surely serve our Father's every purpose in the world.

And how by this same principle will the work of local churches be judged? What kind of church will be successful? They will not be measured by how large they are, or how much money they collect and spend, or how active and efficiently run their program is. No, not even at last by the skill of the preaching. They will rather be judged by the quality of the people they are producing for discipleship in daily living. A local church is a training ground to equip God's people for fruitful service while they grow to maturity in Christ (Eph 4.12–13). When churches do this, every other needful thing will be achieved.

The parable of the *Barren Fig Tree* is both comforting and sobering. In the goodness of God we have another chance if we have been living robotic, fruitless, spiritual lives, but judgment is coming and the axe is lying at the root of the trees. Let no man be presumptuous.

The Great Supper

> Then He said to him, "A certain man gave a great supper and invited many, and sent his servant at supper time to say to those who were invited, 'Come, for all things are now ready.' But they all with one accord began to make excuses…." (Luke 14.16–18)

It was the winter before He died, likely in Judea or Perea, and Jesus was at a large Sabbath feast in the house of an unnamed chief Pharisee. He healed a man suffering from a debilitating heart disease, challenging any to object, but the other guests, eminent people, Pharisees and lawyers, watching Jesus with a critical eye (Luke 14.1) were evidently singularly and astonishingly unimpressed.

And He was watching them, too, observing who was there (not the poor and needy) and how they scrambled for the most prominent seats. Their values were distorted by greed and selfishness. He warned them that this kind of self-exaltation would lead to a humiliating end while a humble spirit would at last bring honor (14.8–11). And He urged them to move beyond their selfish cultivation of a tight circle of relatives and rich neighbors, and reach out to entertain those who in their need were powerless to reciprocate (14.12–14).

It was at this point in the dinner conversation that some well-intentioned but clueless soul observed enthusiastically, "Blessed is he that shall eat bread in the kingdom of God" (v 15). It is not apparent from the text just exactly what kind of bread the spokesman had in mind or how much it still, in spite of all that Jesus had said, spoke of selfish ambition. Perhaps he was just trying rather ineptly to discharge the tension which Jesus' preceding remarks had left at the table. Whatever the case, it is evident from the parable it occasioned that the Lord was not impressed.

The Feast of God

The "certain man" of the parable who prepared a great supper is God. And the parable reminds us that the feast of love and joy which God wishes us to share with Him has been long in preparation. It is the "kingdom prepared… from the foundation of the world" (Matt 25.34) and now "in the fullness of time" (Gal 4.4) God has come to live among His people and invites us to come and rejoice with Him! It is the feast of all feasts. If you never attend another supper, this is the one you must not miss.

And yet those first invited are indifferent! The parable speaks to how little, in spite of their words, the scribes and Pharisees valued the kingdom of God. It also explains why Jesus was most frequently found among people most unlike themselves—poor and desperate outcasts.

The kingdom of God is a kingdom of grace. Those who fill their lives full will have no room nor longing for the bread of God. In their smug self content they will on the other hand receive the invitation of heaven with the gladness of the desperate.

An Incredible Response

The first said to him, "I have bought a piece of ground, and I must go and see it. I ask you to have me excused." Still another said," I have bought five yoke of oxen, and I am going to test them. I ask you to have me excused." Still another said," I have married a wife, and therefore I cannot come" (Matt 14.18–20).

The response of this man's neighbors and friends is both unnatural and improbable. People just do not spurn at the last minute a great dinner prepared at great expense by a man of wealth and importance for the pleasure of his friends. Every lesser matter would be cleared from the calendar and nothing save an "act of God" would keep them away. That is exactly how those invited to the feast at which they and Jesus were now sitting had behaved. The guests cherished the honor being done them and found the chief seats to be a source of special distinction. They had no doubt come on time and thoroughly prepared. It is, therefore, inconceivable that any guests so invited would excuse themselves. It was an absurd situation and it was to reveal it as such that Jesus framed this parable.

The situation in the parable corresponded exactly to the situation of the nation of Israel. They, like the men of the parable, had been told long since by the prophets of the coming of the kingdom of God and like these men they were being told of its immediate approach by the preaching of both John and Jesus "the kingdom of heaven is at hand" (Matt 3.2; 4.17). And yet for all their supposed delight in that kingdom, when the reign of heaven came near, they were wholly unwilling to receive it. In fact, as the present situation demonstrated, they could sit down with its very King and not know it!

Prepared for His Presence

The parable of the *Wedding Garment* (Matt 22.1–14) is so like the parable of the *Great Supper* that some have erroneously judged them to be the same parable differently reported. They do bear on the same theme in a strikingly similar way, but their emphasis is different. Both parables portray the kingdom of God as a joyous feast. Both speak to Israel's contempt for God's goodness and their favored position. Both speak of God's grace toward the "unworthy" and the kind of people most likely to receive His kingdom with joy. But the parable of the *Wedding Garment* adds contemptuous violence and murder to the heedless discourtesies highlighted in the *Great Supper* and contains ominous warnings of harsh retribution. This is not surprising in a parable spoken in the waning hours of the Lord's last week, and may well refer to the brutal Jewish persecution about to break out against Him and His followers. It was a severe warning at a critical time.

In the parable of the *Wedding Garment*, the feast is elevated from just a rich man's social occasion to the wedding feast of a king's son, a once-in-a-lifetime affair. And with this change is even more greatly emphasized the size of the affront offered by the originally invited guests and the dimensions of its consequences. The king could not tolerate this wanton contempt for his sovereignty—the more so because his servants were not sent to collect some onerous taxes but to issue a gracious invitation. In the first parable they merely miss the feast; in the second they forfeit their lives (Matt 22.7). As Hebrews has it, "How shall we escape if we neglect so great a salvation?" (Heb 2.3; compare 10.28–29).

The one thing, however, that stands out and gives a special identity to this parable is not the behavior of those who did not attend, but that of one who did, the man without a wedding garment. The nature of his case has been long debated by students of the parables. It has seemed incongruous to some that the king should be so sensitive about the dress of a ragtag group of diverse people collected from the streets (Matt 22.10)! It somehow clashes, in their minds, with the generous invitation extended to people of every stripe. Where would such people, hastily summoned, have found such robes?

All this has caused many commentators to conclude that the robes were provided by the host and left even the very poorest or hastily invited without excuse. Whatever the circumstance, the man in question found no justification for himself and was summarily cast out for that very reason (Matt 22.12–13). This case makes clear that casual treatment of the kingdom of God, whether by those who never receive it or by those who do, will bring swift retribution. Contempt is contempt. Indifference is indifference. Can those once saved be lost? This parable answers with a clear affirmative. Let no man presume upon the grace of God (Rom 6.1).

It need not be said that even in our democratic age you do not come into the presence of royalty heedlessly. You must be coached in the proprieties of dress and conduct. That is true many times over for those who propose to stand in the presence of the living God. One must clothe himself in the submissive spirit of reverential awe if he proposes to eat bread in the heavenly kingdom. We may indeed not be able to present to Him the sinless life He truly deserves, but the sorriest among us is absolutely able to bring a single-minded and obedient devotion. It is true that in His mercy God has clothed His people with a righteousness not their own, but there is an attitude of heart which we alone can achieve. In the language of the apostle Paul, "Therefore, as God's chosen people, holy and dearly beloved, clothe yourselves with compassion, kindness, humility, gentleness and patience..." (Col 3.12). Such a spirit grows out of the realization that we are always in the presence of the great King and need to be dressed for the occasion.

The thought of divine wrath is fearsome. In preaching, it is sometimes neglected altogether. But both the "feast" parables emphasize it. In the first, the host is angered by the contemptuous rejection of his kindness and declares with finality that "none of those men who were invited will taste my supper" (Luke 14.21, 24). In the second, the wrath of the king towers. Furious with those who had disdained his feast and brutalized his messengers, he sends his armies to destroy both them and their city (Matt 22.7; a reference to the destruction of Jerusalem?). And if the punishment of the man without the wedding robe seems tame by comparison (Matt 22.13), it must be remembered that Jesus frequently used these very words to describe the judgment of the wicked (Matt 8.12; 25.30). They are ominous with eternal anguish.

Inexcusable Excuses

One can feel the anguish of rejection that moves through Jesus' parable of the *Great Supper* (Luke 14.16–24). The excuses made at the last minute by these long invited guests are politely couched but filled with indifference. They are not only uncaring about the pointless effort and expense their late refusal has put their thoughtful host to, but they are insulting. It was a social cut of the most flagrant and unthinkable kind—the sort of thing a man would never do in the world of practical affairs. And probably by design, the response of the reluctant guests in this parable was in stark contrast to the jubilation that must have greeted the invitations to the feast at which Jesus' hearers now sat. Such excuses would have been unthinkable. Invited to the house of a *chief* Pharisee! Allowed to rub shoulders with the rich and powerful! Privileged to share a feast of wonderful food! There must have been a stampede. What an honor! What an opportunity! Forget the land. Forget the oxen. Forget the wife! But of course the Pharisee's feast was of the sort that suited their taste—prestige and pleasure.

There are two possible approaches to these excuses, neither of which is flattering. They could have been lame inventions. As has been frequently suggested, what man would buy a piece of property without first looking it over; and what man would purchase five yoke of oxen without first testing them for soundness; and what man would find a wonderful feast an onerous violation of his duty to his new bride (Deut 25.4)?

But there is another equally damning possibility, and we think more likely. The three men truly intended to be about those things for which they asked to be excused. The new land owner may well have wanted to look again at his property to assure himself that his first judgment was accurate and to better plan its future usefulness: or perhaps like Nebuchadnezzar he simply wanted to savor his achievement (Dan 4.28–30). The buyer of five yoke of oxen is not poor and the purchase could have been made by a servant whose judgment in the matter he now wished to verify by putting them to work adding to his wealth. Business is business. And the bridegroom may have simply chosen to insult his friend rather than to spend one evening away from his new wife.

There was nothing illicit about these preoccupations, but none had any urgency about them either. They worked to reveal in a powerful way what to these men was more important than the one who had invited them to his feast.

"So the servant came and reported these things to his master. Then the master of the house, being angry, said to his servant, 'Go out quickly into the streets and lanes of the city, and bring in the poor and the maimed and the lame and the blind'" (Luke 14.21). It is no wonder that the host of the feast was angry. His supposed friends had pretended great interest in his invitation when it was first issued but at last, when all the extensive preparations were made, they had no time for it. What selfish, insensitive thoughtlessness!

But the investment of the disappointed host will not be wasted. He quickly makes arrangements to fill his house with the poor and afflicted people of the city who from their humble station would find such an invitation almost too wonderful to be true.

"And the servant said, 'Master it is done as you commanded and there is still room.' Then the master said to the servant, 'Go out into the highways and hedges and compel them to come in, that my house may be filled'" (Luke 14.22–23). When those invited from the city streets did not suffice to fill every seat, the servants were sent out to the countryside to urgently invite people at even a greater distance from the host. He wanted his house filled! The only compulsion suggested here is the persuasion necessary to overcome the skepticism of such people that they were really being invited.

The excuse-making guests represented the very people to whom Jesus addressed this parable—the religious fat cats of the temple and synagogue that talked so much of the kingdom of heaven and actually had no interest in it (John 6). They did not cease to be religious, but all their religious posturing was but a subterfuge for pride and worldliness.

The poor and disabled of the city likely represented that large number of Jews whose sins and failures had humbled them, made them desperate and open. Those from the highways and hedges may suggest the Gentiles, a people apparently far away from God but who were to prove more ready to receive Him than the Jews.

Blessed indeed are those who "eat bread in the kingdom of God" (Luke 14.15) but woe to the man who thinks he will sit down at that table not having loved heaven's kingdom above all else.

Someone Truly Cares for You

While David was in unwilling exile from his people, hiding like an animal in the wilderness from a Saul gone mad with jealousy, he composed these plaintive lines: "For there is no one who acknowledges me... no one cares for my soul" (Psa 142.4).

The truth is that Someone did and does care. The people who most often crowded longingly around Jesus during His days of teaching were the throwaways—that large group of men and women who knew well their own moral and spiritual failures and were made to feel them even more keenly by a religious elite who saw them as worthless and unworthy. Jesus touched them powerfully because He so obviously valued and cared for them even as He called on them to repent and follow Him.

Such was the case when Jesus taught that well known trilogy of parables concerning lost things which Luke alone records (Luke 15). (Matthew does place the story of the lost sheep in an earlier discourse on humility, Matt 18.12–14.) Large crowds of the great "unwashed" had come to hear Jesus preach while a small knot of increasingly antagonistic Pharisees grumbled their disdain of "this man" who "receives sinners and eats with them" (Luke 15.2). Jesus paused in His teaching to answer again His critics who in their blindness kept on repeating a charge which not only commended the Lord but severely indicted them.

Jesus preached the gospel of the kingdom not as to those who had, as they imagined, made themselves *worthy of it*, but as a door opened to all. The message of the Pharisees was a message of reformation in order to be worthy at last for a call to the kingdom. The gospel of Jesus was to sinners as they were, promising forgiveness and a welcome to every believing, penitent heart. Actually, as the first two parables bear out, Jesus was worse than the Pharisees had made Him out. He not only received sinners but went looking for them!

There is no doubt that these three parables about lost things and lost persons are principally addressed to the attacks of the Pharisees. They begin most emphatically as an appeal to human nature. They contain the "what would you do?" kind of argument which the Lord frequently used (Luke 14.5). What would any shepherd do if he lost a sheep? What would he do if he found it? And what would a housewife do if she lost some money? And what would she do if she found it? Everything about these illustrations is so natural as to need no explanation. All people, even Pharisees, long after lost things and rejoice greatly when they are recovered, even things as mundane as a sheep or a coin. Implicit in His argument is, surely a human being, however degraded, is worth that much!

Even more probing Jesus is asking, what would you do if you lost a son? What would you do if you found him again? And, if you were where God is and had lost all these "children" what would you do? And how would you feel if they came home again? If you don't understand what I am doing, try understanding yourselves!

This was Jesus' parabolic defense of His concern for the moral recovery of the degraded and His belief that it was absolutely possible and worthwhile. To His critics the tax collectors and "sinners" were only insignificant bits of hopeless human refuse toward whom they were indifferent. Incongruously these human beings, made in the image of God, were worth less to the Pharisees than an ordinary sheep or a day's wages. For them they had no concern and no joy. These parables say that it was the behavior of the Pharisees that was unnatural, even subhuman, and not that of the Lord.

In the third and most powerful of His three parables Jesus moves from the defense of His own misunderstood love to the rebuke of the Pharisees lack of it. He has shown them how they should have been; now He will show them how they are. The focus of the parable of the *Prodigal Son* is not on the "prodigal" but the elder brother who portrays in such dark and tragic ways the attitude of the self-righteous scribes.

Yet even in this story of severe rebuke there is love and entreaty toward those for whom it is intended. It is an invitation to joy, an invitation to share His and the Father's love for lost men and women of all kinds; but there is a hard and humbling road which they must walk before they will be ready to receive it. And before it is over they will be dismayed to learn that those whom they have so despised had already made the journey before them.

In these parables, perhaps more than any other, is revealed the real work and purpose of the kingdom of heaven. To lose this focus upon lost people, the earnest searching to find them, the wholehearted joy at their return, is to lose the Christ who taught them.

The Shepherd and His Sheep

Shepherds and sheep were such a familiar part of the ancient world that they became a ready metaphor for biblical writers. The shepherd's tender care for his sheep moved David and his fellow psalmists to speak of the Lord as Israel's shepherd (Psa 23; 80.1) and Israel as "the sheep of his pasture" (Psa 100.3; 95.7; 79.13; 78.52).

The prophets also in their messianic visions saw God in a similar way: "He will feed his flock like a shepherd, he will gather the lambs in his arms, and carry them in his bosom, and will gently lead those that have their young" (Isa 40.11); "I myself will be the shepherd of my sheep, and I will cause them to lie down, says the Lord God. I will seek that which was lost, and will bring back that which was driven away..." (Ezek 34.15–16).

Old Testament writers also made effective use of the well known disposition of sheep to stray off. Of our sinful ways Isaiah wrote, "All we like sheep have gone astray" (53.6) and the longest of the Psalms closes with this plaintive appeal: "I have gone astray like a lost sheep; seek your servant; for I do not forget your commandments" (119.176).

In His illustration of the shepherd and the sheep (Luke 15.3–7; Matt 18.12–14), Jesus was not only approaching His hearers from known practice but with a familiar biblical metaphor. There was no way for them to miss the lesson. Jesus, as did His Father, saw men as "weary and scattered, like sheep having no shepherd" (Matt 9.35).

Sheep are usually lost through their own carelessness. Forgetting both fold and shepherd they wander aimlessly with nothing more in mind than the next clump of grass. There is no thought of wolves or steep precipices. How accurately this mirrors our own inept ways. It is not that we one day make up our minds to be ungodly and then begin methodically to fulfill our ambition. We are merely so preoccupied with present desires and circumstances that we become heedless of the consequences of our choices. Lives lived without purpose make us pawns of our passions and, whether by design or no, we find ourselves before we know it far from God, miserable in our helplessness and hurt. Such sheep do not represent the proud and stubborn but the hapless, those who are quick to own their stupidity and sin but are nonetheless lost.

But the focus of the parable is the shepherd. Arguing from the lesser to the greater, Jesus takes the known attitude of a shepherd toward lost sheep to justify His attitude toward lost people, and to expose the merciless spirit of His critics. He had earlier made the same kind of argument from a physician's attitude toward the sick (Matt 9.12). The Pharisees knew that no true shepherd would ever abandon a lost sheep even though the rest of his flock was secure. With shepherds the concern was not merely economic, but sentimental. They would often grow so attached to the sheep as to call each by its own special name (2 Sam 12.3; John 10.3).

The Pharisees also knew that the shepherd would not, upon finding his sheep, pummel it in anger, but bear the now severely weakened stray gently on his shoulders. Furthermore, when he returned, he would return with open gladness.

By this simple illustration Jesus raised an implicit question with His detractors—why they could have such compassion for a sheep and treat men with such arrogant and self-righteous harshness. They not only had not sought the lost sinner but would not rejoice at his recovery. And in this they had dramatically shown how their own disposition differed from the divine one. While God rejoices, they sulk. While Heaven forgives, they spit their contempt. While the good Shepherd seeks to recover the scattered flock, they live to ravage it. It is a dark picture.

But some may be puzzled by Jesus concluding observation, "there will be *more joy* in heaven over one sinner who repents than over ninety-nine *just* (righteous) persons who need no repentance" (Luke 15.7). Is He suggesting that God feels a lesser joy over the righteous than the recovered sinner? Two things. The joy of recovering the lost is a special kind of joy, a joy filled with relief, but it never precludes as deep a delight in that which has never been lost. And, the term *just* or *righteous* which Jesus uses here has a special ironic twist to it. Who in the world would be so righteous as to need no repentance? Unfortunately, the Pharisees thought they could tell you. The truth is that all the sheep have strayed (Rom 3.9–10) and need the mercy of "that great Shepherd of the sheep" who redeems us "through the blood of the everlasting covenant…" (Heb 13.20). This great Shepherd will "gather the lambs in his arm, and carry them in his bosom, and will gently lead those that have their young" (Isa 40.11).

The Ever Seeking Savior

> Or what woman, having ten silver coins, if she loses one coin, does not light a lamp, sweep the house, and search carefully until she finds it? And when she has found it, she calls her friends and neighbors together, saying, "Rejoice with me, for I have found the piece which I lost!" Likewise, I say to you, there is joy in the presence of the angels of God over one sinner who repents. (Luke 15.8–10)

In this second of three parables, which Jesus used to justify His gracious pursuit of sinners, He uses the same argument from ordinary life as in the parable of the *Lost Sheep*. "What woman...?" We know, He says, what any woman who had lost a silver coin in her house would do. She would scour the whole house; turn it upside down until she found that lost coin.

It is important for us in thinking about this parable not to imagine that we are dealing with some woman of wealth, or that the coin is similar in value to our modern ones. The lost coin was a Greek *drachma*, the equal of the Roman *denarius*, and equivalent to a day's wages in the ancient world (Matt 20.1–2). It would have been a serious loss to the average household in a world where existence was often hand-to-mouth and one coin made the difference between survival and desperation. In just such a household Jesus had been born and reared. Even in our comparative affluence, there are few of us who wouldn't search our houses diligently to find a misplaced sum of money equal to a day's income and feel delighted and relieved when it was recovered.

Some have speculated that the lost coin may have been one of the ten silver coins customarily given by a bridegroom as a frontlet for his bride. Such a coin would obviously hold sentimental as well as practical value. Its loss would compare to the loss of a wedding ring, which holds symbolically within it all the remembered promises and joys of a marriage. Of this possibility, we can only say that nothing in the parable either forbids or establishes it.

The focus of the parable of the *Lost Coin*, like that of *The Lost Sheep*, is on the natural concern for things lost and the joy of recovering them. There is no justification for allegorizing this story which, taken as it is, makes Jesus' point admirably. Fertile imaginations have seen the woman (or the house) as a symbol for the church; the lamp as a figure for God's Word, and the sweeping of the house as a sign for the disturbing work of the Holy Spirit. As Buttrick observed concerning some of Trench's treatment of the parable, "it is an allegorizing we may gladly ignore."

It is dangerous to make this parable walk on all-fours. An inanimate coin, lost due to the carelessness or misfortune of others, obviously falls woefully short of perfectly symbolizing animate and free-willed man. Caught up in the very error he warns about, Buttrick writes at length about people who are lost because they are born to cruel circumstances and cannot help being where they are. Nothing could have been further from the Lord's mind. He is appealing for a repentance which, though it leads to mercy, demands unequivocal acceptance of responsibility for one's transgressions (Luke 13.3, 5). How can one turn away from that which he did not choose?

This parable, like the former, is not just about divine mercy but about the unquenchable longing in the heart of God for every sinner, the sense of loss that sends Him searching. This mercy is more than available; it is passionate in its determination to recover every person which sin has denied Him. Francis Thompson portrays this relentless pursuit in his very personal poem, "The Hound of Heaven":

> I fled Him, down the nights and down the days;
> I fled Him, down the arches of the years;
> I fled Him, down the labyrinthine ways
> Of my own mind; and in the mist of tears
> I hid from Him, and under running laughter
> Up vistaed hopes I sped;
> And shot, precipitated,

A down Titanic glooms of chasmed fears.
From those strong feet that followed, followed after.

As Barclay has observed, no Pharisee had ever dreamed of a God like that. One perhaps that would be merciful to the good who came to plead deserving ways, but certainly not one who would go in search of society's worthless scabs. But there was nothing in Jesus' ways the Pharisees could not have anticipated had they ever truly understood the God of the Old Testament on which they had so long doted. From the Garden of Eden to the last plaintive appeal of the prophets, He had been in relentless pursuit of His lost people—however sorry their state, however indifferent their response. Unlike the woman in the parable, Jesus will never recover all that are lost to Him, but it will never be for lack of seeking and searching.

Parable of a Loving Father

> And then He said: "A certain man had two sons. And the younger of them said to his father, 'Father, give me the portion of goods that falls to me.' So he divided to them his livelihood. And not many days after, the younger son gathered all together and journeyed to a far country, and there wasted his possessions with prodigal living." (Luke 15.11–13)

The parable of the *Prodigal Son* is the concluding and most moving of the three parables which Jesus taught in defense of His treatment of sinners. It could better have been called the parable of the Loving Father than that of the Prodigal Son because it opens up the heart of God as surely as it exposes the thoughts of sinful men. Moreover, it was the older son rather than the younger whom Jesus wished his critics to see, for like him they were as lost as the "sinners" they despised, but in their arrogant self-righteousness did not know it. They were, in fact, the real prodigals. In this parable Jesus proposes to assure scorned sinners of the greatness of God's forgiving love and to rebuke into repentance the sanctimonious humbug of their detractors.

This parable is a moving story of a father's love for his two lost sons, and is intended to make us feel his anguish, and his joy. A lost sheep and a lost coin can, once found, be easily put right, but what do you do with a stubborn, rebellious son? You can replace a sheep or a coin, but how do you replace a lost child? "Lost" and "found" reach their greatest intensity in this final story.

The younger of two sons, contemptuous of his father and determined to lead a life of his own, demands ahead of time his part of his father's estate (one third, Deut 21.17). His pride and rebellion have driven out all thought of his father's goodness or the heartbreak his departure will bring. For the moment he is utterly full of himself. It is not a pretty picture.

Amazingly enough, the father, knowing full well the boy's folly, gives him his inheritance and watches him go, confident, ungrateful, and heedless of what was ahead of him. We may wonder why the father did not stop his son. The reason is simple: he did not because he could not, for in his heart the boy had already left, was already in the "far country."

The prodigal doubtless took his journey fairly intoxicated with his new found freedom. He must have had intentions of sooner or later making his mark in the world but with no one to account to and no one to care, he quickly ran through his inheritance in an orgy of carnality, and the freedom he had exulted in soon turned to the most abject kind of slavery. A sudden famine reduced him to the ultimate degradation (for a Jew)—tending swine for an uncaring man who kept him in a state of half starvation. The far country took all he had and gave nothing. The very freedom that had seduced him has now virtually destroyed him. He is the lowest of all servants.

This young man is a perfect model of humanity's self-willed course. We too have received a rich heritage from God—healthy bodies, good minds, loving relationships, a beautiful world. He has given "us richly all things to enjoy" (1 Tim 6.17) with only one proviso, that we should gratefully acknowledge Him for His goodness. And what have we done? We have taken those gifts as though they were ours by right and wasted them in enterprises that were either sinful or meaningless. The "far country" is not a place but an attitude. It is the mindless arrogance that says we don't need the God who created us and we are tired of His meddling in our lives. So we declare independence from the One who gives us "life and breath and all things" and set off on our own. It may be possible to be more stupid than that but it is difficult to imagine it. It was in just this way that Paul describes the degradation of the ancient Gentile world. "… Because although they knew God, they did not glorify Him as God, nor were they thankful, but became futile in their thoughts and their foolish hearts were darkened" (Rom 1.21).

The "prodigal son" is frequently seen as a stand-in for drunks, drug addicts, and sexual athletes. But this is a mistake. There are a lot of upstanding prodigals who waste the gifts of God in a "respectable" pursuit of wealth or power or human wisdom. Lives are thrown away in plush offices as often as on skid rows. You can find the "far country" in a lot of places.

Sin is a waste. It takes everything precious and irreplaceable and devastates it. And this happens because we try to seize our lives for ourselves instead of yielding them up to the one who has in his goodness given them to us in the first place (Matt 16.25).

The Insanity of Sin

> "But when he had spent all, there arose asevere famine in that land, and he began to be in want. Then he went and joined himself to a citizen of that country, and he sent him into his fields to feed swine. And he would gladly have filled his stomach with the pods that the swine ate, and no one gave him anything. *But when he came to himself,* he said, 'How many of my father's hired servants have bread enough and to spare, and I perish with hunger! I will arise and go to my father and will say to him, "Father; I have sinned against heaven and before you, and I am no longer worthy to be called your son. Make me like one of your hired servants."'" (Luke 15.14–19)

How meaningful in His story of the prodigal is Jesus' use of the expression, "he came to himself." The boy had literally been "out of his mind" in his efforts to run from his deeply caring father. It was self-will not sanity that drove him to the far country. Intoxicated with the thought of absolute freedom He fled his father's love and wisdom. He was not running *to* something but *from* something, and in doing so he far overestimated his own abilities. It was an insane adventure that wound up costing him heavily. And yet it was altogether predictable.

The same may be said of us when we set out to get away from God and His "onerous" restrictions. Sin makes no sense. A man cannot win in a war with God. You cannot find happiness by trying to become something that God did not make you to be. It is madness to try. The thought that we are powerful and wise enough to recreate ourselves in an image of our own choosing has got to be the height of both arrogance and folly.

For some time, however long, the prodigal endured the degradation of the pig pen. Perhaps he tried to convince himself that it was only a temporary setback and that those pigs didn't really smell as badly as they did. But any hope that some of his "good time" friends would deliver him was quickly shattered ("no one gave to him"). His employer, a hard and ungracious man with far more concern for his pigs than his workers, was also a dead end street. It became quickly apparent that someone as hungry as he was, was ready to eat pig fodder and in no position to save himself.

The ambitious young man who had gone forth to make his mark in the world was now utterly helpless. He had come to the end of his tether.

Reality has a way of rising up and smacking us in the face and most of us have to be smacked hard before we get rid of our delusions and start seeing the obvious. The prodigal first faced the practical fact that his father's common laborers were eating far better than he was. He then faced the greater truth that his father truly loved him and that he had treated him with contempt. It was the latter realization and not the former that at last changed him. One can imagine the flow of tears as he grappled fully with what he had done. The fact that he had blown his whole inheritance and reduced himself to utter degradation was the least of his blunders. The unwarranted grief and anguish he had caused his father was the true crime. Grief stricken and blaming no one but himself he resolves to go to his father, confess his sin, declare his unworthiness, and ask for a job as a common laborer. Pride is broken. Humiliation has become humility.

Some cynics might argue that the boy just did what he had to do in his circumstances, but that is not true. He had other options. He could have just toughed it out, stolen, sold a pig on the side, and blamed his troubles on everyone else but himself—his father, his friends, his employer. It's done all the time. To his great credit he chose not to do that. It's hard to face up to your folly, but it is insanity not to. We, too, can choose to ignore reality, eschew blame, rail against God or others but sin is a hard taskmaster and there will be no mercy. "The way of the transgressor is hard" (Prov 13.15). The hard won "wages of sin is death" (Rom 6.23). "There is no peace, says the Lord, for the wicked" (Isa 45.22).

This world is an insane asylum where men and women are delusively seeking escape from the realities of God and their own nature (Rom 1.21–22). Those who awaken in brokenhearted penitence to humbly serve and glorify their Creator are the ones who have returned to their senses.

You Can Go Home Again!

Thomas Wolfe was right in one way when he wrote those memorable words, "You can't go home again." Things on the material plane are always changing. People die. Buildings fall to ruin. Green fields are paved over. But he was wrong in the ultimate sense. We can return to our heavenly Father's house. That is always presumed in the parable of the *Prodigal Son*. The emphasis of the parable is on those attitudes which either send us home to God or keep us away.

The father of the prodigal did not step in to save his wayward boy from the consequences of his foolishness. He let him take every blow that his witless choices had brought him, with the hope that hard experience would succeed where wise counsel had failed. This kind of love is not easy. It is instinctive for parents to spare their children pain, but far better brief pain than endless agony. In the same spirit God subjected the creation to vanity… *in hope* (Rom 8.20). Many parents today could find a lesson in this story. Love must sometimes be tough. You cannot coddle children into godly character and love. Only the humble godliness of parents expressed in patient but uncompromising discipline offers any hope of succeeding.

Does God send difficulties our way when we turn away from Him? He may not have to since our own silliness seems to bring plenty of heartache and misery on its own. But God's love is such that He certainly wouldn't work to turn Manasseh from his orgy of idolatry, God sent him to Babylon in chains, which did (2 Chron 33.10–13). So also with the prodigal. With a far clearer vision of his father and his father's house and heart broken in repentance, he turned resolutely homeward. The one who left demanding "give me…" now returns pleading "make me…" What a difference attitude makes!

The Homecoming

"And he arose and came to his father. But when he was still a great way off, his father saw him and had compassion, and ran and fell on his neck and kissed him" (Luke 15.20). The return of the prodigal apparently did not catch the father by surprise. Not because he often thought cynically, "Just wait, the fool will come running back here with his tail between his legs," but because there would have been few days that he did not look longingly down the road where with breaking heart he had last seen his son's retreating silhouette. He saw him "when he was still a great way off" because he was looking for him, hoping for him, longing for him. This father did not stand waiting with offended dignity. He ran to him and kissed him repeatedly. (See Luke 7.38 for same Greek verb.) There were no comments on his pathetic appearance; no berating words about the hurt his departure had caused; no sermons on the duty of good sons. Even the boy's carefully planned words of penitence were left incomplete by the father's interrupting call for the rejoicing to begin.

What a picture of God this is. Will God run, you ask? The ancient philosopher who observed that great men don't run had a perverted sense of greatness. Great men especially run. They run heedless of all but the need of others. They run in joy and compassion. And God, who, greater than all, runs to meet all who are coming to meet Him. Remember, "God *so loved* the world...."

Doesn't God rebuke, you say? Yes, He does, but only those who are not already heartbroken with their sinful unworthiness. For the true penitent there is no reproach (Jas 1.5); only reassuring mercy and encouragement.

I think it is safe to say that the returning prodigal was stunned by his father's reception. He had doubtless prepared himself for the worst and in his most optimistic dreams had never imagined this. Perhaps for the first time he realized how much his father loved him. It certainly never entered his head to say, "This is going to be easier than I thought." Only people who do not know what they have done and what they deserve would entertain such a dishonorable thought. He knew. He knew very well. And for that reason there was no room in his heart for anything save amazed gratitude for his father's extravagant love.

And so the party began. What rejoicing! What inexpressible exultation! The father's most earnest longing had come true. Nothing is spared, "for this my son was dead and is alive again; he was lost and is found."

How powerfully Jesus reveals the heart of God toward sinners in this simple but compelling story. God, He is saying, cares for His prodigals just like we care for ours. And we are compelled to say, "Yes, Lord, even more—even far more."

The Prodigal Who Stayed at Home

> "Now his older son was in the field. And as he came and drew near to the house, he heard music and dancing. So he called one of the servants and asked what these things meant. And he said to him, 'Your brother has come, and because he has received him safe and sound, your father has killed the fatted calf.' But he was angry and would not go in. Therefore his father came out and pleaded with him." (Luke 15.25–27)

It is here that the plot of the parable of the *Prodigal Son* thickens. The setting of Jesus' story makes it evident that however moving the saga of the younger son, the older son is the true focus of the parable. It was told in response to the self-righteous charge of the Jewish religious elite that Jesus exposed His true character by the company He kept notorious "sinners" and scoundrels. Their accusation actually did more to reveal their own sanctimonious and merciless pride than any flaw in the Lord, a fact they were unlikely to notice. And it was out of concern for them, not the "sinners" they despised, that this great parable arose—a story about a wastrel son, a brokenhearted father, and a brother who refused to be reconciled to either. How could they possibly not be touched by this compelling story of a father's love for a wayward son and his rejoicing at his recovery? Weren't they fathers, too? Isn't this what they would have done?

The older son does not seem at first to play much of a role in the story. When his father at his brother's request divides his property, he simply receives the two-thirds of his father's wealth which was, as the firstborn, due to him (Deut 21.17). If he shared his father's heartbreak at his brother's abrupt departure or his anxious longing for him while he is gone, we are not told of it. He was tending to business on the farm. While his witless brother was wasting good money in a wild revel, he was the soul of industry.

He was respectable and responsible. His brother was unforgivably worthless. He was good, his brother bad. In this contrast, the elder brother found his sense of meaning and value. It was what made his world orderly and sensible.

But now suddenly all that order comes crashing down. His wastrel brother has returned; not to shame and disgrace, as he surely deserved, but to music and dancing! The anger of the older brother ran white hot at such injustice. For his diligence and faithfulness there had been no rejoicing and festivity, not even a skinny kid goat! But now, for this worthless whoremonger, an ecstasy of joy! It was absolutely and unalterably wrong.

His father's entreaty for him to come in and join the rejoicing was for him an invitation to soft-headed stupidity. His father was as big a fool as his brother was a profligate. It was a violation of all that was fair and right and he was not about to have a part in such insanity. In his reaction he not only shows his contempt for his once wayward brother, but for his ever faithful father. For the man who reared and gave him all he had there is neither respect nor compassion. His arrogant self-righteousness ("I never transgressed your commandment at any time") and self-serving ambition are left rawly exposed. It was an ugly scene; and Jesus meant it to be.

The boy who stayed at home was as much a prodigal as his younger brother. He had lived all this time eating the dry husks of self-righteousness while, as his father reminded him, "all that I have is yours." It was not his worthiness that would have provided this abundance, but his father's love. All he had ever needed to do was ask.

This great parable is a portrait of two figures: God in His great goodness and mercy and the Pharisee in his wretched spiritual miserliness. Like the elder brother, the Pharisee did not serve God because he loved Him but because it brought him some sense of overwhelming personal superiority. He was abjectly poor in his imaginary worthiness when he could have been rich in God's grace. As the elder brother viewed his younger brother, the Pharisees looked with disdain on socially disgraced "sinners" and never saw their own spiritual poverty. The truth is that they were worse by far than the publicans and "sinners" with which they accused Jesus because those outcasts frequently knew and readily acknowledged their sinfulness—something of which no self-respecting Pharisee would ever have been guilty. Therefore, as Jesus once told them, "The tax collectors and harlots enter the kingdom of God before you" (Matt 21.31). And yet God loves them, and pleads with them also to come to the party. What a great Father!

Parable of a Shrewd Scoundrel

> He also said to His disciples: "There was a certain rich man who had a steward, and an accusation was brought to him that this man was wasting goods. So he called him and said to him, 'What is this that I hear about you? Give an account of your stewardship, for you can no longer be steward.' Then the steward said within himself, 'What shall I do? For my master is taking the stewardship away from me. I cannot dig; I am ashamed to beg. I have resolved what to do, that when I am put out of the stewardship, they may receive me into their houses.'" (Luke 16.1–4)

So begins Jesus' parable of the *Unjust Steward*. This parable is without doubt the most controversial of the Lord's parables. Emperor Julian the Apostate used it to attack the ethics of Jesus. More sympathetic students, intimidated by Jesus' use of such an unsavory character to teach his lesson, have tried to "save" it by fanciful interpretations. Anselm thought it an illustration of the rise, progress, and fruit of repentance (clearly the farthest thing from the unjust steward's mind). Schliermacher with as much unlikelihood supposed the master to symbolize the Romans; the steward the publicans and the debtors the Jewish people—the point of the parable being that graciousness by the publicans toward their own people would at last bring praise from the Romans and a warm reception by the Jews. Another saw the master as God and the steward as the Pharisees who, for their own advantage, sought to diminish the real demands of God from His people (Matt 19.3–9; Matt 23.16–18). But what could possibly be commendable about that?

The weakness in all such interpretations is a failure to realize that parables are not allegories but tend to focus on a single point of comparison and the rest just fills out the story.

There is no question that the central figure in the parable is an unmitigated scoundrel. Jesus Himself calls him "unjust" (Luke 16.8). The implication is that his squandering of his master's goods was more from greed than ineptitude. He is also an insufferably proud and self-pitying little rascal when found out—"too weak to dig and too proud to beg" (but not to steal!). Living off the sweat of other men's labors would appear to have made him both soft and vain; and his method of bailing himself out of the difficult circumstances that his own dishonesty put him in? More of the same. Evidently he was not able to cover himself by "cooking the books." He simply sought to ingratiate himself to his master's debtors by allowing them to fraudulently rewrite their notes. One got off with more than 400 gallons of oil and the other with above 200 bushels of wheat. And if these debtors knew what was going on they were hardly better than their benefactor.

Admirable?

The most astonishing thing to most is the master's response to the steward who had squandered his wealth and more recently robbed him further. He "commended his unjust steward because he had dealt shrewdly" (Luke 16.8). But nothing more should be read into this than a grudging admiration for the deft way the steward had wriggled out of a bad situation. He was not only slick, he was farsighted and resourceful, and singularly focused. Unfortunately, these were skills which he turned to his own rather than his master's advantage. He simply recognized clearly what was ahead of him and acted judiciously to save his skin. Any good crook would have done the same. The question is: in what way can this unprincipled man's behavior provide any useful model for the Christian?

First Jesus commends, not his character, but his shrewdness. "For the sons of this world are more shrewd in their generation than the sons of light" (16.8). The steward was surely a "son of this world" for his perspective was entirely carnal. He was a rascal but he was a wholehearted rascal. Jesus' point is that if ungodly men can focus so intently and shrewdly on worldly aims, why can't God's people wholeheartedly make all their resources serve eternal ends (Eph 5.8–14)? In short, that cheat of a man judges those

Christians who invest the bulk of their physical resources and time in here and now enterprises. Like the unjust steward, we rob the real Owner of that wealth which we only hold in trust.

Jesus' counsel is to "make friends for yourselves by unrighteous mammon [wealth], that when you [mg. it] fail, they may receive you into an everlasting home" (16.9). The identity of such friends would not be hard to come by. And how do we do this? By putting our very temporary material resources to godly ends that enter into eternity and make us like the One who said, "I go to prepare a place for you... that where I am there you may be also" (John 14.2–3; see Matt 6. 19–20).

The Wickedness of Neglected Opportunity

In the parable of the *Unjust Steward* Jesus seems to introduce a theme which He carries into His story of the *Rich Man and Lazarus*, i.e., we must make the present serve the future. The former parable was spoken to His disciples but He now directly addresses the Pharisees who, notorious for their covetousness (Matt 23.14), have been listening to His applications of that parable with contemptuous derision (Luke 16.14). The stirring story that Jesus tells is a living demonstration of the principle that Jesus had just pressed upon these worldly and often immoral hypocrites: "For what is highly esteemed among men is an abomination in the sight of God" (Luke 16.15).

> There was a certain rich man who was clothed in purple and fine linen and fared sumptuously every day. But there was a certain beggar named Lazarus, full of sores, who was laid at his gate, desiring to be fed with the crumbs which fell from the rich man's table. Moreover the dogs came and licked his sores. (Luke 16.19–21)

There has been considerable discussion whether the story of the *Rich Man and Lazarus* is history or a parable. It is unique in that one of its characters is named and in that it is not a story of familiar things calculated to illustrate unfamiliar truth. The story seems to be its own message, one that uniquely comes from beyond the grave. We conclude that it is both history and a special sort of parable (cf. R. L. Whiteside, *Bible Studies*, Vol. 4, p. 424). We strongly disagree with A. B. Bruce who refers to the story as "fictitious history."

The opening scene of this story is a silent tableau, a study in stark contrast between two men: A rich man who is lavishly clothed, housed and fed, and whose life is one of unbroken sumptuous living, and a beggar named Lazarus whose weak and ulcerated body compelled him to depend upon others to lay him at the rich man's gate where he fed along with the dogs on scraps thrown from the rich man's table. The Greek word translated "to be fed" has the root meaning of feeding fodder to animals and came to be used of humans in a contemptuous way. His name, the Greek equivalent of the Hebrew Eleazar (God is my helper) seems belied by his wretchedness or perhaps speaks the truth of his man-forsaken state. Lazarus was just a part of the landscape which the rich man saw every day but did not see.

Though Lazarus is very much present in the story, it is obvious that the wealthy man is the central figure. There is no indication that the rich man was dissolute, dishonest, or miserly, or that Lazarus was ever driven from his gate. Lazarus was just the ever present opportunity which his unintended benefactor, busy with his own carefree life, never noticed. And that, at last, was his wickedness. One marvels how it could have happened, but it is done every day by ordinary people, blessed in life, who at first notice and are touched by the miseries of others, but then are occupied with their own interests, cease to notice and to care.

The moral and spiritual character of Lazarus is never discussed because it would have made no difference to the principle of compassionate love being illustrated by its utter absence. The beggar's spiritual condition is left to be implied by what happens in the afterlife: "So it was that the beggar died, and was carried by the angels to Abraham's bosom. The rich man also died and was buried" (16.22).

No matter how people may fare in life, death is always democratic—one death for each of us (Heb 9.27). So Lazarus, weak and ill, at last expired. His death and absence from the gate no doubt went as unnoticed as his presence. There is no mention of his burial. The final end of a penniless beggar in society might easily be imagined—dumped unceremoniously into some potter's field. Then, the rich man also died. He was buried, likely in the tomb of his fathers, and carried there with great ceremony by a great crowd of friends and minions. But they went with him only so far. As for Lazarus, unnoticed as he might have been by men, he was borne by the angels of God into the afterlife. For the rich man there were no angels. Already we are getting intimations of how this story is going to end. Circumstances in this life certainly do not portend what may lie ahead. We all need vision with a greater reach.

Two Men Went Up to Pray

> And he spake also this parable unto certain who trusted in themselves that they were righteous, and set all others at nought: Two men went up into the temple to pray; the one a Pharisee, and the other a publican. (Luke 18.9–10, ASV)

Though the service of the temple was almost exclusively sacrificial, public prayer as well as private devotions had grown up around the offering of the morning and evening sacrifices (Luke 1.10; Acts 3.3; 10.30; Josephus, *Antiquities*, xiv, 4.3). Just such an occasion had drawn to the temple the two men of this parable. They entered together but in attitude and position they were a universe apart.

Two Men

That the scene of this parable is as old as history is evident from the story of Cain and Abel who also went up to worship God (Gen 4). The Pharisee, like Cain, was quite willing to go up to worship but like his ancient prototype he did not take God seriously. There was no room for the holiness and greatness of God in a mind so fascinated with its own significance. Religion for such men becomes a vehicle not for awe-inspired worship but for self-elevation. The Pharisee in this parable represented the worst features of that exclusivist Jewish sect, never likely exceeding 5,000–6,000 members, which held itself apart from others as the sole practitioners of the law of God. The truth was that they tortured the law with ridiculous extrapolations and invalidated it with their own traditions (Mark 7.1–23; Matt 23.1–26). Theirs was a formula for religious pride and hypocrisy but, generally esteemed by the people, they would have been first called on for prayer in a crisis.

The publican, on the other hand, was part of a heartily despised group of infamous Jews who had "sold out" to collect taxes for the Roman invaders and, having provided the revenue which their contract with Rome required, they characteristically enriched themselves further by mercilessly squeezing the people for even more. Hated for their greed as well as their treachery, they were classed with the heathen and the greatest of sinners (Matt 18.17; Luke 15.1–2).

Two Prayers

In the Pharisee's "prayer" never was thanksgiving ever uttered with less gratitude. He speaks not of God's mercy but of his own merit and instead of an address to God it is a soliloquy of self congratulation. But even if all he said of himself were true (and the Lord does not challenge it) it was far from enough. He says nothing of covetousness and lust or generosity and mercy. The Sermon on the Mount would have torn him up. His "excellence" consists not in pleasing God but in being so much better than the "dogs" around him. His "righteousness" was not a function of his relationship to God but of the wickedness of others. As much as he despised the publican, he needed him to enlarge his own sense of worthiness. He could have viewed the agonized publican with compassion but instead looked on him with contempt. Having no sense of his own failures he had no compassion for his failed brother. Like Cain, whose irreverence for God made brotherly love impossible, he saw all others as unworthy and hopeless.

The Pharisee asked for nothing because he felt no need, confessed no sin because he felt no guilt. He stood in a gold mine and admired the rocks. He had nothing because he asked for nothing (Jas 4.2). What a misbegotten use of religion!

The publican's prayer was brief but to the point. He addresses God with reverent desperation. His prayer is honest and humble, a recognition of the immensity of his failure, and a longing to be different. He calls himself not "a sinner" but "the sinner" as if to acknowledge the greatness of his sins (see 1 Tim 1.15). Unlike the Pharisee, he is too crushed by his own iniquity to be aware of that of others. He needs God's mercy and pleads for it.

The Conclusion

The result of the two prayers is poetic. The man who felt so full left empty. The man who felt so empty left full. Justification is God's gift to the humble and contrite, and it comes with the assurance of a transformed life. Pride always leads to destruction.

We may ask if we never get beyond the need to hit rock bottom, to have to face up again to our desperate need for God's mercy. Hopefully, we can avoid the moral and spiritual crashes that bring us to the ground, but we will never grow beyond our daily need for God. Contrition will likely be our daily bread as we strive honestly to live beyond past failure. This is what growing into the image of Christ is all about.

Whatever Is Right

> For the kingdom of heaven is like a land owner who went out early in the morning to hire laborers for his vineyard. Now when he had agreed with the laborers for a denarius a day, he sent them into his vineyard. And he went out about the third hour and saw others standing idle in the marketplace, and said to them, "You also go into the vineyard, and whatever is right I will give you." So they went. Again he went out about the sixth and the ninth hour, and did likewise. And about the eleventh hour he went out and found others standing idle, and said to them, "Why have you been standing here idle all day?" They said to him, "Because no one hired us." He said to them, "You also go into the vineyard, and whatever is right you will receive." (Matt 20.1–7).

So begins Jesus' parable of the *Workers in the Vineyard* which, recorded only by Matthew, was likely spoken in Perea (Matt 19.1) during the last months of the Lord's life.

This story is to some the most challenging of all Jesus' parables and it does contain some puzzling elements that seem to defy the ordinary realities of human nature. It helps to remind ourselves that His parables characteristically contain two elements: (1) a situation that occasions it, and (2) a story which teaches a single lesson. The task of the student is to find the message in the parable which harmonizes with the circumstances which produced it.

The grape harvest came in Palestine in late August or early September and had to be gathered before the mid-September rains. There would, therefore, at times have existed the kind of urgency that demanded many workers. A denarius a day was a common wage for day laborers who were customarily hired at dawn and paid at day's end. The hand to mouth life they lived meant that the failure to find work one day could mean hunger for the next. For this reason the law strictly forbad holding back a worker's wage (Deut 24.14–15).

The story at first appears to be ordinary. A vineyard owner goes out early to contract a group of workers for a denarius a day. Finding the original hire inadequate he returns four times to look for more—at 9, 12, 3, and finally 5 o'clock when the work day is nearly ended. These latter workers who had before waited jobless were simply told by the owner that he would give them "whatever is right" (vv 4, 7). They evidently agreed gladly. Some work is better than none.

So far, so good. But things begin to take a strange twist at pay time. The workers were paid in reverse order of their being hired and the ones who worked only a partial day were paid the same denarius as the contract workers who had been at the job from sunrise. One can imagine what was going on in the heads of the contract labor as they watched in surprise at what was given those who came late. What will we be paid? Twelve denarii?! Four? Two?

Expectations must have floated skyward. And then the jolt. They were paid just exactly what they had bargained for… but now it seemed terribly unfair and they complained bitterly to the vineyard owner of the inequity of being paid the same as men who had worked only one hour! (vv 8–12). The disciples, listening, were likely sympathetic; even we could be tempted.

This is no ordinary farmer, and evidence for their commonality in New Testament times is lacking. He is certainly not money wise. A few episodes like this and he will be out of business. He would have driven a financial adviser crazy! This man seems to be more concerned with the needs of the workers than what they had actually earned. They were not shiftless, but unemployed, and he knew what disappointment and suffering would come when they returned home with a sum far too small to feed their children.

But was he fair to his contract laborers? Had he cheated them in being gracious to the others? His answer to their grumbling is as firm as it is logical: "I am doing you no wrong. Did you not agree with me for a denarius? Take what is yours and go your way. …Is it not lawful for me to do what I wish with my own things? Or is your eye evil because I am good?" (vv 13–15).

What is the lesson of this story? It is not the length of time we serve the Lord but what we produce for Him that counts? There is no evidence of equal productivity in these workers. All the Lord's disciples will receive the same reward? True (Eph 4.4), but is that the message of this parable?

The occasion that produced this unusual story and the context that surrounds it must determine the answer.

The Great Reversal

Jesus' parable of the *Workers in the Vineyard* (Matt 20.1–15) has been frequently given interpretations that ignore its context. Irenaeus thought it revealed God's one divine purpose in all the different calls to righteousness from Adam through the apostles. Chrysostum saw it as encouragement for those called to Christ late in life. Calvin viewed the parable as a warning against careless overconfidence. Some see the workers' equal pay as a lesson in salvation by grace. Others discern a prophecy of the rejection of the Jews in favor of the Gentiles.

But what does the context tell us? The parable was clearly occasioned by Jesus' exchange with the rich, young ruler (Matt 19.16–22) who found himself unwilling to give up all for the kingdom of God. The Lord's observations about the difficulty with which the rich come to the kingdom startled the disciples who thought wealth a sign of divine favor. From all this Peter was stirred to ask what he and others who had left all for Him should expect to receive (19.27). Another conspicuous contextual clue is the statement which both precedes and follows the parable (19.30; 20.16): "So the last will be first and the first last."

In responding to Peter's question, Jesus answers both the question and the spirit in which it was asked. Peter was likely as pleased with the Lord's reference to the apostles sitting on twelve thrones "in the regeneration" as he was ignorant of its meaning. The apostles had been for months perversely fascinated with which one would be "greatest in the kingdom" and this same chapter tells of a carnal effort by James and John to elevate themselves above others (20.20–21; Mark 10.35–37). They were yet to understand the "cup" for which they lusted (Matthew 20.22–23) or the "thrones" on which they longed to sit (Matt 16.19; John 20.22–23; Acts 2.42). In much suffering they were destined to speak the words of Jesus by which the world would be both judged and saved.

To Peter's question Jesus answers that those who have given up "houses or brothers or sisters or father or mother or wife or children or lands" for His sake would receive "a hundred fold now in this time—houses and brothers and sisters and mothers and children and lands [referring to the loving fellowship of the saints, Acts 4.32; Rom 12.10, 13]—and in the age to come, eternal life" (Mark 10.29–30).

To Peter's hireling spirit Jesus responds with a parable which speaks of two, and only two, different groups—the "first" and the "last."

It is on the contrasting attitudes of the workers who were hired first and those hired later that the parable focuses. The first hired represent those who look to themselves and the value of their work for justification with God and feel they have made themselves more deserving by their long and arduous labor—so much work, so much pay. They got what they bargained for.

Those hired later in the day reflect the men and women who have in their desperate need set their hope not on themselves but on God. They believe Him to be both fair and merciful and that He will give not what is deserved but what is needed. He has saved His people "not by works of righteousness which we have done, but according to His mercy..." (Titus 3.5).

These two groups of workers represent the proud and self-reliant and the humble and self-emptied (Prov 16.18–19; Isa 57.15; 1 Pet 5.5). The proud will try to seize the kingdom by force (by contract), and the humble will receive it as an undeserved gift. The self-righteous hirelings will be ungrateful toward God and without compassion for others (The first-hired workers could have been grateful for enough at day's end and glad for the happy circumstance of their struggling fellows but they were not.). They typify those who see all that God gives them as their right and their relationship with others as a struggle for dominance. In difficult times they are likely to become bitter and complaining, hard to correct. Their labor in the kingdom may be grudging and their disposition to self-righteousness great.

The workers who in their need simply trusted the vineyard owner for whatever He might give are the humble and undeserving who are profoundly grateful for God's goodness, compassionate toward others, contrite when wrong, joyful in their labor for the Lord, and deeply concerned to please Him in all things (Isa 66.1–2).

But is it wrong for Christians to look toward heaven? Not if they realize that all they receive will be by grace, and that the true reward is being with Him, working for Him, and becoming like Him (Rom 8.28–30).

And to whom is the parable directed? Toward all who like Peter are dreaming of some great reward for some great thing done. He had to be reminded that even the greatest of sacrifices without love achieves nothing (1 Cor 13.3).

It is not how great the labor but how true the heart that makes one "first" in the kingdom of heaven.

The King is Coming—What Then?

> A certain nobleman went into a far country to receive for himself a kingdom and to return. So he called ten of his servants, delivered to them ten minas [pounds], and said to them, "Do business till I come." But his citizens hated him, and sent a delegation after him, saying, "We will not have this man to reign over us." (Luke 19.11–14)

Thus begins Jesus' parable of the *Pounds*. It is similar to the parable of the *Talents* but delivered at an earlier time, a different place, and with a slightly different emphasis.

As Jesus began His last journey to Jerusalem, excited Passover pilgrims were speculating over whether He would come to the feast and what would happen if He did (John 11.55–57). His enemies they knew were plotting against Him, but what power He had and what wisdom!

In the midst of this ferment, while passing through Jericho, Jesus related the parable of the *Pounds* to bring the misguided enthusiasm of His followers into check. "Now as they heard these things, He spoke another parable, because he was near to Jerusalem and because they thought the kingdom of God would appear immediately" (Luke 19.11).

The parable of the *Pounds* is a familiar story of the fortunes and trials of the nobility and of the work and responsibility of the slaves who served them. Both Herod the Great and his son, Archelaus, had received kingdoms from Rome in just this way. It was also not uncommon for citizens to rebel against rulers imposed on them from afar. From such well-known happenings Jesus sought to teach His disciples that not only was final victory not at hand but that the struggle of His kingdom was just beginning.

The Lord is clearly seen in the nobleman who went away to receive a kingdom (Dan 7.13–14). It was a kingdom which was

162 | *Glimpses of Eternity*

to begin now (Acts 2.32–36) but whose final triumph would come later (1 Cor 15.24–26).

The sum the departing nobleman settled on each of his ten servants (slaves) was the same. It was neither inconsequential nor impressive. In New Testament times money circulated simultaneously from Roman, Greek and Jewish sources. The mina, a Greek coin equal to a hundred Roman denarii, would have represented less than a third of a year's earnings by an ordinary laborer.

It seems a small sum from a man about to receive a kingdom but may have been chosen to make a needed point for Jesus' disciples and hangers-on—it is the cross before the crown; humble service before exaltation.

In addition to his servants, the noblemen had also to deal with a rebellious citizenry. From the two, Jesus intends in His parable to bring to a sobering accountability both His disciples and His enemies. The latter are seen in the religious elite of Jericho who had drunk deep of Pharisaic hypocrisy and were scandalized by Jesus' entrance into the home of a notorious chief publican. Yet it was Zacchaeus, the "sinner," who proved to be a true child of Abraham. The former were the multitudes who had followed Jesus with growing excitement and admiration to Jerusalem, fully confident that the kingdom of God was about to break forth in worldly power and splendor. One group was nobler than the other, but neither understood fully what the Lord had said to Zacchaeus: "The Son of Man has come to seek and save that which was lost" (Luke 19.10).

For His followers Jesus counsels the patient commitment of their lives to the task with which He Himself had been invested—the salvation of men.

Instead of some quick and easy victory He speaks of arduous labor ahead—a labor which will test their devotion to Him and work to shape their characters for His return in glory.

Christians have a momentous stewardship for which they must at last give account (perhaps the gospel which, given "in trust," must be faithfully delivered to others as received, 1 Tim 6.20; 2 Tim 1.13–14; 2.2). Those who have served faithfully will be rewarded (the parable with its earthly setting speaks of earthly rewards but the Christian's hope is reserved in heaven, 1 Pet 1.4). Those who fail their stewardship through indifference or fear of failing will be pronounced "wicked" and lose their place in Christ's service entirely (Luke 19.20–24). Those who have rejected His rule out of hand will die before the king (2 Thes 1.7–9).

A startling paradox, "I tell you that to everyone who has shall more be given, but from the one who does not have, even what he has shall be taken away." *So* Jesus defends the nobleman's taking of the mina of the "wicked" servant and giving it to the servant who had gained ten. Remember, the money was not theirs but a stewardship from their master. Individual disciples and churches should remember that God will not give more opportunity to those who fail to seize what they have. The reward of the faithful is more work to do.

Facing the Bottom Line

Parable of the Two Sons

During the last week before His death, the parables of Jesus become more urgent—more filled with ominous warnings of judgment.

On Sunday the Lord had entered Jerusalem to an acclaim which stunned and offended the Pharisees (Luke 19.39). On Monday He infuriated the Jewish establishment by again driving from the temple the traders who fed like vultures on those who came to worship (Mark 11.15–19).

On Tuesday, profoundly stung, His enemies came at him in waves. The first were the Jewish leaders who interrupted His teaching with a challenge to His authority: "By what authority are You doing these things? And who gave You this authority?" (Matt 21.23). Not a bad question, honestly asked, but there was no genuineness in this inquiry. They were going to kill Him whatever He said but they wanted desperately to first discredit Him with the people. "These things" likely had more reference to His tumultuous entrance into the city and His peremptory expulsion of the traders from the temple than to his teaching. And the "authority" that concerned them was likely more civil than divine. They wanted a copy of His parade permit!

Frankly, this was a rather pointless question to raise with one who with their full knowledge had recently brought to life a man four days dead! Moreover, He had given them His authority: "It is written, 'My house shall be called a house of prayer, but you make it a den of thieves'" (Matt 21.13).

To expose their hypocrisy, Jesus refuses to answer until they deal honestly with John's baptism, whether it was from heaven or from men.

Trapped by their own duplicity and unable to answer either way without painful consequences, they pretend not to know and fall into an embarrassed silence. Their insincerity made them unworthy of an answer. But Jesus is not through with them.

It was on this occasion that Jesus told the brief little parable of a father who had two sons. "But what do you think? A man had two sons, and he came to the first and said, 'Son, go, work today in my vineyard.' He answered and said, 'I will not,' but afterward he regretted it and went. Then he came to the second and said likewise. And he answered and said, 'I go, sir,' but he did not go. Which of the two did the will of his father?'" (Matt 21.28–31). Reminiscent of the much longer and more detailed parable of the *Prodigal Son* which defended God's grace toward sinners in the face of Pharisaic self-righteousness, this parable, powerful in its simplicity, goes directly to the critical question of obedience.

The meaning of the parable in this setting is quite clear. In the first son, rebellious and ungrateful in his refusal to work in the very vineyard which supplied his living and was destined one day to be his, is seen the publicans and other socially reprehensible sinners. They were extravagant in their rejection of God until John brought them to repentance and Jesus transformed their lives by His spirit and teaching. The second son, overtly polite and submissive but in fact uncaring and disobedient, perfectly represents the scribes and Pharisees who were as short on performance as they were long on profession. Reaching for the jugular, Jesus asks His detractors which son obeyed his father, and they, finding no place to hide, reluctantly and likely in a whisper said, "the first." But Jesus does not relent. He presses His point with words that must have surely cut the Jewish leaders to the quick, "Assuredly, I say to you that tax collectors and harlots enter the kingdom of God before you. For John came to you in the way of righteousness, and you did not believe him; but tax collectors and harlots believed him; and when you saw it, you did not afterward relent and believe him" (Matt 21.31–32). John had come pressing sincerely what the Pharisees professed, prayer (Luke 12.1) and fasting (Matt 9.14), but unmoved they dismissed him as demon-possessed (Matt 11.18). And even when they saw the worst of sinners whom they despised responding in humble repentance to John's preaching they were unrelenting in their stubbornness (Luke 7.29–30).

What are the lessons of this parable? That God is gracious to those who though grievously disobedient in the past penitently turn to do His will, but that He has no patience with the ritually repeated professions of those who never deliver the goods. That preaching and praying and singing way beyond what we are willing to live is a travesty of righteousness. That those who do nothing about the truth already made available to them are unworthy of any more whether sinner or saint. That honesty in dealing with ourselves and God is critical to the practice of the Christ-like life. How sad to be among those who live in such insincerity that they are unable ever to know the truth about God or themselves.

The Danger of Despising God's Goodness

Jesus holds back nothing now. His time, before awaiting, is here (John 2.4; 7.6, 8; 12.23). He has come to Jerusalem to die and both His deeds and words are designed for confrontation. The Lord, having led the Jewish leaders into judging themselves disobedient to God with His brief parable of the man with two sons, will not let them go, but presses His point even further with a parable which forces them to decide the punishment their disobedience deserved. They have expressed concern about authority. He shows them that true authority is the last thing on earth they are concerned about.

> Hear another parable: There was a certain landowner who planted a vineyard and set a hedge around it, dug a winepress in it and built a tower.
> And he leased it to vinedressers and went into a far country. Now when the vintage-time drew near, he sent his servants to the vinedressers that they might receive its fruit. And the vinedressers took his servants and beat one and stoned another. Again he sent other servants, more than the first, and they did likewise to them. Then, last of all, he sent his son to them, saying, "They will respect my son." But when the vinedressers saw the son, they said among themselves, "This is the heir, Come, let us kill him and seize the inheritance." So they took him and cast him out of the vineyard and killed him.
> Therefore, when the owner of the vineyard comes, what will he do to those vinedressers? (Matt 21.33–40; note also Mark 12.1–9 and Luke 20.9–16)

This story was familiar in a troubled land full of vineyards and absentee owners. The landlord had planted his vineyard and provided everything necessary to make it fruitful—a wall to keep out predators, a tower from which to guard it, and a rock hewn winepress in which to receive and process the grapes. He then let out the vineyard to others for a share of the produce.

These tenant farmers, either overly impressed with their own investment or become unscrupulously ambitious, determined to refuse the owner his rightful return and seize the vineyard for themselves. Messengers sent to them were abused and killed, and finally the owner's son is murdered. Though A. B. Bruce finds the behavior of the vinedressers unbelievable, William Barclay says it was not unknown in the explosive Palestine of the times.

The message of this parable, one of the few recorded by all three synoptic writers, seems abundantly plain. More allegory than parable, the Lord's story gives a thinly disguised history of God's past experiences with Israel and a warning of the ultimate tragedy their hypocrisy was about to work. The prophets had so often compared Israel to a vineyard gone wild (Isa 5.1–7; Jer 2.21; Hos 10.1) that it seems incredible that His hearers did not see where Jesus was leading them. The owner of the vineyard was clearly God.

The vineyard was Israel. The vinedressers were the rulers of the nation who had sought by force to seize the kingdom for themselves. The servants of the owner were the prophets of God who were rebuffed, mistreated, and killed by a recalcitrant nation. The beloved and only son of the owner was Jesus. A true heart could have saved the Jewish rulers but dishonesty was driving them to ever greater excesses.

God's patient love is powerfully evidenced in this parable. It is seen in the owner's incredible hope that after sending one servant after another to an increasingly brutal reception that just one more might bring a change of heart. He even persists through the unspeakable outrages of his tenants until they have viciously killed his only son. It is not the behavior of the vinedressers that appears inconceivable, but that of the owner!

This parable perfectly reflects Israel's treatment of God's prophets whom He sent to them over many years saying, "Oh, do not this abominable thing which I hate" (Jer 44.4). God's mercy was despised, His messengers persecuted and killed (Neh 9.26).

The vineyard owner in the parable had to know well the risk he put his only son to in a last ditch effort to turn his rebellious tenants. God knew more than risk. He knew the reality of the cross.

Jesus' purpose in this parable was to show the rulers of His people the road they were on and where it would lead. Their hypocritical religiosity merely disguised a seditious desire to seize authority from the true King which would inevitably lead them to destroy their own Messiah. What would the owner of the vineyard do to those miserable tenants, Jesus asked the Jewish leaders. They replied with heedless fierceness, "He will destroy those wicked men miserably and lease his vineyard to other vinedressers who will render to him the fruits in their seasons" (Matt 21.41). Unwittingly they had sentenced themselves. As Jesus would later warn, upon them was to fall "all the righteous bloodshed on the earth…" (Matt 23.35). Their house would be left to them desolate. This parable is full of lessons.

Forgetting Who Owns the World

Jesus' parable of the *Wicked Husbandmen* was a stinging rebuke for first century Jews who had tried to seize the kingdom of God for themselves, but it is an equally powerful warning for inhabitants of the late twentieth century who are still chasing the same illusion.

What does this parable say to us as human beings? We have been blessed by God with such eminent privileges. Life itself is a marvel, but life with an intellect, will, and moral conscience is transcendently remarkable. We are "fearfully and wonderfully made" (Psa 139.14). And God has equipped us to live fully and joyously in this world by "filling our hearts with food and gladness" (Acts 14.17) and giving "us richly all things to enjoy" (1 Tim 6.17).

Moreover, God has determined out of eternity that we, if willing, are to be more than His creatures. We are to be His sons and daughters (Eph 1.4–5), heirs of His glory (Rom 8.14–17).

Yet, discontent and ungrateful, and filled with an inflated sense of our own importance, we, like the ancient Jews, have tried arrogantly to take control of our lives and seize the credit for whatever good there is in them (Rom 1.21).

The question is: What is the vineyard of God for us? What gift of God have we tried to take for ourselves? Is it lifestyle or future plans, a cherished career, our family, our image, money, property? And when did the transition from His to mine take place? Nothing happens so easily and so subtly as people who live and function in a world created and maintained by God beginning to think they own it all or ought to. Call it the god-complex of the Garden of Eden, (Gen 3.5–6) or a gargantuan case of denial, we have the power to convince ourselves of the impossible! Thoughts of how hard we have worked for what we have, or how much we deserve, or what we are on the verge of achieving, begin to dominate. We begin to begrudge even the little service we give God as if it were some undeserved gratuity, and we think of Him only in crisis times when the vineyard of our lives bears no grapes. It is an ugly picture and unconscionable.

What makes things even more incredible is the fact that those to whom the parable was first addressed were "devoutly" religious! None therefore should pay more careful attention to the lessons of the parable than those who see themselves as servants of God. Is it Christ who rules in our local churches or some mindless "democracy" which allows no disconnect from our own agenda and the worldly culture in which we live? Have we very cleverly dispossessed the Son of God from His church and seized it for our own without concern for the fact that He is both its owner (Matt 16.18) and its head (Eph 1.22–23)? The world is full of "Christians" who want nothing to do with the Jesus of Scripture and in their own refined way murder Him afresh.

The patience of God with such foolishness is the only thing which exceeds our folly. As already noted, it is the behavior of the vineyard owner of the parable that shocks us. What landowner would put up with even the tiniest bit of such brutal arrogance?! For ourselves we must ask just how many of God's entreaties for change (through His word, others, or provident circumstances) we have rejected.

Our behavior in God's "vineyard" whether it is His creation or His church, should always acknowledge His ownership and sovereign rule. Our refusal to submit to and live within such obvious truth fills with absolute equity the righteous judgment of God upon us (Matt 21.40–46). As Paul has observed, emboldened in our wickedness by God's patience, we simply store up for ourselves "wrath in the day of wrath and revelation of the righteous judgment of God" (Rom 2.4–5). The very thought of such should to be a reality check for people both religious and irreligious.

Perhaps as Lloyd John Ogilvie has suggested, we should take another look down the road from our vineyard and see who is coming still in His righteousness and grace to receive His own. Mercy unspeakable is giving us another opportunity to open our life to its true owner. Now we can finally say what we have in our sinful stubbornness formerly refused to say: "Lord, this is your vineyard, this is your life. It has never belonged to me though I have acted as though it did. Please forgive my sinful foolishness. Yours is the kingdom, world without end."

God's Goodness and Severity

On Tuesday, in His temple confrontations with the Jewish hierarch, Jesus in a third successive parable continued his ever increasing theme of judgment. In the parable of the *Wedding Feast of the King's Son* (Matt 22.1–14), as in the parable of the *Wicked Vineyard Keepers*, the patient goodness of God is illustrated but only to highlight the wicked contempt of His enemies and to justify a severe punishment.

Jesus had been pointed in applying to His enemies the harsh judgment they themselves had rendered against the vineyard keepers (Matt 21.41). Like rebellious builders, He said they were rejecting the very stone whom God intended to be the head of the corner (Matt 21.42; Psa 118.22–23) and were destined to stumble over it and be crushed into powder by it. The kingdom in which they took such pride was to be taken from them and given to those who understood and practiced its righteousness (Matt 21.43–44). Enraged, the chief priests and Pharisees had only been restrained from seizing and killing him by fear of a popular reprisal (Matt 21.46; note John 11.47–53).

The parable of the *Wedding Feast* gives no relief. It is an even more intense parable of indictment and judgment, a stern warning of disaster.

> The kingdom of heaven is like a certain king who arranged a marriage for his son, and sent out his servants to call those who were invited to the wedding; and they were not willing to come. Again he sent out other servants, saying, "Tell those who are invited, See, I have prepared my dinner; my oxen and fatted cattle are killed, and all things are ready. Come to the wedding." But they made light of it and went their ways, one to his own farm, and another to his business. And the rest seized his servants, treated them spitefully, and killed them. (Matt 22.2–3)

The king in this parable is unbelievably gracious. The long invited guests who flatly refused when first summoned to the wedding of the son of an oriental king (an occasion of state) would have been fortunate to escape with their lives after such a political affront. Imagine what Ahasuerus would have done to any of his ministers who refused his invitation to dinner (Est 1.3)! Instead, the king sends other servants to entreat further and even graciously entice them with the rich feast he has prepared. Openly contemptuous, most proceeded to more appealing business while some outraging all civility terrorized and murdered the king's servants. In the former parable the workers disdained their duty. Here the king's subjects despise not only his power but his goodness. One wonders how they thought to escape the consequences of such raw effrontery. The stage is set for judgment.

"But when the king heard about it, he was furious. And he sent out his armies, destroyed those murderers, and burned their city" (Matt 22.7).

A. B. Bruce has correctly suggested another difference in the parables—the previous one approaching the history of Israel from the Old Testament perspective of prophets rejected and killed before the Son was finally sent and murdered, and the second from the New Testament perspective speaking of the rejection of the invitation to the kingdom first issued by John, Jesus and His disciples, and then finally by the apostles after Jesus' death and resurrection.

The nation of Israel was the object historically of so much grace, so many second chances. But that has been true for us all. And that goodness and mercy so often rejected, Paul warns, enlarges the righteousness of God's wrath and judgment. "Or do you despise the riches of His goodness, forbearance, and long-suffering, not knowing that the goodness of God leads you to repentance? But in accordance with your hardness and your impenitent heart you are treasuring up for yourself wrath in the day of wrath and the righteous judgment of God" (Rom 2.4–5).

It is a grave mistake to "make light" of the kingdom of heaven and to give great weight to matters of limited significance. This was the sin of most of the Jews, and most of us—too busy with momentary matters to accept God's invitation to the truly great joys. But the Jewish establishment was not indifferent; they were murderous. Of those who brutalized and murdered the king's messengers, Jesus says that the king "destroyed those murderers, and burned their city." Is it possible that though certainly speaking to their eternal end (Matt 23.33), He has reference to the calamitous judgment in history about to be brought on Jerusalem? His words later the same day would indicate it. "Therefore, indeed, I send you prophets, wise men, and scribes: some of them you will kill and crucify and some of them you will scourge... that on you may come all the righteous bloodshed on the earth. ...Assuredly, I say to you, all these things will come upon this generation" (Matt 23.34–36. Note also 24.1–34).

So with us, too. Whether by cold indifference or harsh opposition, if we reject the kingdom of God our house will be left to us desolate, both here and hereafter. The God who is love (1 John 4.8) is also a consuming fire (Heb 12.29).

Underdressed at the Wedding Feast

The Judgment of Grace Abused

Some think that Jesus' parable of the *Wedding Feast* is actually two parables spoken at different times and joined by Matthew, but the parable's unity of both narrative and theme make that extremely unlikely. The parable begins with the judgment of grace despised and concludes with the condemnation of grace abused (A. B. Bruce).

> Then he said to his servants, "The the wedding is ready, but those who were invited were not worthy. Therefore go into the highways, and as many as you find, invite to the wedding." So the servants went out into the highways and gathered together all whom they found, both bad and good. And the wedding was filled with guests. (Matt 22.8–10)

Since the "worthy" guests (divinely chosen but faithless Israel) had proven themselves "unworthy," the king determined to find replacements anywhere and everywhere. Irrespective of character or station his servants invited both the "bad and good," the reputable and disreputable (no man is "good" in the ultimate sense, (Matt 19.17). They were the "unworthy" who made themselves "worthy" by an attitude of joy and gratitude at an honor so incredibly gracious. They were "worthy" because they knew they were not (Luke 7.6–9).

Without doubt, the diverse multitude invited to the wedding feast represented those the Jewish establishment found so unworthy, i.e., everyone else—Jewish outcasts. Samaritan "dogs," and pagan Gentiles. This parable foreshadows the statement of Paul and Barnabas to the blasphemous Jews of Pisidian Antioch: "It was necessary that the word of God should be spoken to you first; but since you reject it, and judge yourselves *unworthy* of everlasting life, *we turn to the Gentiles*" (Acts 13.46).

But just as the parable seems to be coming to its natural conclusion, the palace filled with enthusiastic guests, Jesus introduces a new element into his story. "But when the king came in to see his guests, he saw a man there who did not have on a wedding garment, so he said to him, Friend, how did you come in here without a wedding garment? And he was speechless" (Matt 22.11–12).

The king's attention is drawn to the man without the wedding garment not because he was on an inspection tour, but because his dress, totally inappropriate for the occasion, stood out like a sore thumb.

And when he had no explanation for this affront, the king's response was not gentle—"bind him hand and foot, take him away, and cast him into outer darkness; there will be weeping and gnashing of teeth" (Matt 22.13).

We might be inclined to see this as unduly harsh treatment for so small a slight, and especially when visited on a supposed penniless man who came to the feast gladly but on short notice. But there is no evidence that the people invited were taken directly to the palace without time to prepare or that they were all poor and variously disabled as in the parable of the *Great Feast* (Luke 14.21). The poor and unfortunate were in all likelihood well represented, but they were not targeted nor mentioned and the idea that the king's expectation by way of dress would have been beyond them is presumed. Perhaps it was beyond them, and perhaps as so many have presumed the king had provided the wedding garments, but it is strange that a feature so critical to the story's message goes unnoted.

Whatever the case, the slight was not small. The king took such casual indifference to propriety as a grave insult to his majesty, a concept that may be lost on a generation that seems not to understand that clothes may not make the man but they can make a statement. Jesus is now addressing His disciples who have already answered the call to the "feast." This last scene dramatically stresses that God's grace is not a haven for irresponsibility, but that a Christian is not beyond the loss of heaven (1 Cor 10.1–12; 2 Pet 2.20–22). Those who have been forgiven are expected to live up to the incredible privileges to which a merciful God has called them. We were not invited to the palace so we could behave like mindless clods (Gal 5.13).

What does the wedding garment represent? Not the righteousness, we believe, with which God in His mercy clothes us in our conversion (Rom 3.21–24), more mirrored in the feast itself, but the practical holiness with which we must clothe ourselves as children of a holy God (1 Pet 1.15–19: Heb 12.17).

The open rebels who contemptuously and even rejected the king's invitation are those who fell by self-will and self-righteousness. The man without the wedding garment speaks of those who fall by presumption, who think that the grace of God is an invitation to heedless excess and have not learned what Paul warns of, that more sin does not lead to more grace but to death (Rom 6.1–23).

Lessons from a Wedding

> Then the kingdom of heaven shall be likened to ten virgins who took their lamps and went to meet the bridegroom. Now five of them were wise and five were foolish. Those who were foolish took their lamps and took no oil with them, but the wise took oil in their vessels with their lamps. But while the bridegroom was delayed, they all slumbered and slept. (Matt 25.1–5)

So begins Jesus' parable about ten young ladies who were nearest in the ancient world to our bridesmaids. Matthew places it in the somber conversation which Jesus had with the disciples after His final confrontations with the establishment Jews on the Tuesday before He died (Matt 22–24).

Jesus had shaken His disciples as they gloried in the beauty of the temple by telling them it would be destroyed amidst a great cataclysm of tribulation before the present generation had died (Matt 24.1–35). He then moved to speak of His own coming for which they were to be always prepared because it would be at a time unheralded and unexpected (Matt 24.36–44). It was to be a day, He said, when the master of the house would reward his servants for their faithfulness or punish them for their disobedience and presumption (Matt 24.45–51). Jesus especially warns of the seduction to carelessness which His perceived delay might bring (Matt 24.48).

It was with these warnings still ringing in His disciples ears that Jesus told the story of the wise and foolish virgins. Framed around the most joyful celebration of the ancient world, it yet speaks soberly of how a coming judgment must guide present conduct. And it is a message for His own.

There is some confusion about the exact details of ancient Jewish weddings, and they may well have varied like our own, but Jesus' story would surely have reflected customary practice.

The effort of some commentators to build the whole meaning of this parable on details thinly inferred is unhelpful. Had such details been central to its message, the Lord would certainly have supplied them.

The actual wedding of a couple was preceded by a betrothal so binding that it could only be ended by divorce (Matt 1.18–19). When the time came for the marriage to be consummated the bridegroom would rejoice with his friends and companions for a time (Matt 9.15; John 3.29) and then proceed to the home of the bride. Some have suggested that it was the festive practice for the bridegroom to keep even the day of his coming secret so as to catch the bridal party unprepared; but if so there is no hint of it here. Jesus says that the bridegroom was "delayed," indicating an expected time.

Since oriental weddings were usually celebrated in the evening, the bride's companions (Psa 45.14) waited expectantly for the bridegroom, carrying lamps to light his way to the home of the bride where she would join the bridegroom and proceed to the place of the wedding feast. But, and here the burden of the parable reveals itself, the bridegroom delayed his coming. Wearied with waiting, the bridesmaids at last slept, until suddenly at midnight they were startled awake with the cry, "The bridegroom is coming! Go out to meet him!" Five of the ten young ladies had prudently brought extra oil for their lamps, but five had not. Now, finding themselves embarrassingly unready because the bridegroom's delay had exhausted the oil in their lamps, they pled with their wiser companions to share, and were refused.

It can seem rather selfish and unfeeling for the young ladies who had extra oil to refuse to share with their distressed associates, but their explanation seems more practical than selfish: "No, lest there should not be enough for us and you; but go rather to those who sell and buy for yourselves" (Matt 25.9). To them it presented the prospect of no burning lamps at all. Some have even thought the wise virgins not only selfish but cynical in advising their mates to go and buy oil at midnight, but there is no indication that such was unthinkable or that oil was not found. A. B. Bruce thinks that the oil was not important to the story and that the failure of the foolish bridesmaids was not just in failing to bring more in the first place but in putting so much emphasis on it that they missed the wedding feast. It may seem unthinkable to us that a bit of oil could be that critical at a wedding, but it is the Lord's story not ours, and He is the one who focuses so intently upon it.

It may also seem strange to us that when the bridesmaids returned from a visit to the oil merchant to find the door to the place of the wedding already shut, that the bridegroom himself would refuse their earnest appeals for entrance. Yet there is indication that such was not unknown in the ancient world.

That then is the story but what are its lessons? Our task is to find them.

Lessons from a Wedding (2)

The parable of the *Ten Virgins* is another of Jesus' parables in which the main character is absent until the very end (Matt 22.1–14; 24.45–51). They speak of a judgment to be pronounced on a world from which God is apparently absent and in which, for the moment, we seem able to have our way. They address the temptation that assaults us in our response to this "absent" Deity who has left us with nothing more than a promise that He is coming, that history is not spinning endlessly, but moving inexorably to a grand conclusion when the doors will be shut and the world as we know it will be forever ended.

In all this it is clear that the only thing that can save us is a tenacious faith that pays no attention to the way things look at the moment. He is coming, and He is coming without warning! (Matt 24.36–44). The only question left unanswered is how that fateful moment will find us.

This parable warns that just as the first can be last (Matt 20.16) so those who begin on the inside can wind up on the outside. There is a need for Christians to serve the Lord, not with the mindless notion that there will always be more time, another opportunity, but with a moment by moment faithfulness and constancy. The folly of the foolish virgins was not in a failure to make preparation, not even in a failure to make reasonable preparation. How many weddings wind up taking place at midnight!? Their foolishness was an expression of the wisdom of this world that is moderate about the ultimate and passionate about the inconsequential. Their failure was in not being prepared to meet the bridegroom whenever he came.

Actually it was the wise young ladies who probably looked unfashionably foolish as they carried about their spare containers of oil. And so today truly devoted Christians are destined to appear to the world, and even to thoughtless disciples, as mindlessly conservative, needlessly restrictive, altogether too focused on one thing. This parable says that even Christians, like convicted but disobedient sinners, can choose to live their lives as if, contrary to both reason and faith, present circumstances will always prevail—no testing, no death, and no judgment. It makes us pathetically vulnerable to being overwhelmed by unexpected temptation, unanticipated tragedy, or, most tragically, sudden death or the Bridegroom's swift and unheralded return. The Lord has not just warned that the unexpected *may* happen in regard to His coming. He has absolutely declared that it *will* happen. "Therefore... be ready, for the Son of Man is coming at an hour you do not expect" (Matt 24.44).

The oil for the lamps in this wedding party does not stand for justifying good works or some mystical spiritual power but for faithfulness, for attendance upon whatever is necessary to strengthen ourselves against unexpected temptation or tribulation (a life of trust and dependence on God and the constant companionship of godly people) and to prepare ourselves to meet the Lord in peace (faithful attention to godly Character and behavior and to the tasks to which He has called us). More is required of the Lord's disciples than an occasional panic stricken "fearful expectation of judgment." His will and character must so take root in us that they are always essentially present and we will always be found *as we are* whenever our Savior bursts suddenly and finally upon the scene of history.

A subsidiary lesson of the parable is that our responsibility in Christ is like our relationship to Him—personal. We cannot be lit vicariously by the spiritual light that burns in others. There is no way to borrow a pure heart or a godly character in a crisis. Such things cannot be rented or suddenly passed on. They have to be personally chosen and cultivated. Parents cannot fail for years to train their children in righteousness and then expect some godly individual to magically deliver them in a moment from disaster. We cannot live our lives with indifference to eternal things and expect our way through the valley of shadow to be lit by the oil of others' faith. The righteousness of others will not save us in the judgment (Ezek 14.14; 18.20).

The crisis of this parable is obviously of small consequence. The lives of the bridesmaids were not going to be wrecked over one missed wedding. And besides it may seem to us that the story lacks credibility because the bridegroom would surely have opened the door to the entreating latecomers. But it is the Lord's story and the crisis it illustrates is ultimate. The time comes when the great plan of God for His people will joyfully culminate in the wedding feast of the Lamb (Rev 21); and what exultation there will be for those who are ready to meet Him! But, as this parable ominously warns, what darkness and emptiness awaits those found outside when that door is finally and forever shut (Matt 22.13). Jesus' simple story speaks powerfully of both heaven and hell.

The Man Who Would Not Try

> For the kingdom of heaven is like a man traveling to a far country, who called his own servants and delivered his goods to them. And to one he gave five talents, to another two, and to another one, to each according to his own ability; and immediately he went on a journey. Then he who had received the five talents went and traded with them, and made another five talents. And likewise he who had received two talents gained two more also. But he who had received one went and dug in the ground, and hid his lord's money. And after a long time the lord of those servants came and settled accounts with them. (Matt 25.14–19)

In this way Jesus begins His parable about three bondservants entrusted by their master with the investment of his money. Though it is not possible to know this with certainty, it may have been His last parable. In Luke's account, Jesus' parables come with a rush during the last few months before His final visit to Jerusalem and then die away to only one in the last week. The reverse is true of Matthew who gives us only one in the last months and then, suddenly, in a single day of the last week, a quick barrage. In them He stresses His impending departure followed by a return in judgment at a time uncertain.

It was Tuesday of the Lord's last week (Matt 26.1), a day in which He had the last confrontation with His enemies. This parable, however, like the one which precedes it (the Ten Bridesmaids), is spoken not to His enemies but to His disciples. It is a lesson to Christians.

Jesus' "for" in beginning the parable of the *Talents* indicates that it builds on the point of comparison already established in the preceding parable. That parable spoke of an unexpected delay in His coming and the critical importance of a complete and constant readiness.

Nothing should be presumed. This new parable addresses itself more to how we should spend the intervening time when the Lord delays His coming ("After a long time the lord of those servants came"). The servants, unlike the bridesmaids, are not just to wait but to work, and as stewards of the goods of another to give account. And they are not hired servants but slaves, bondservants, who are not even in possession of their own bodies. Yet they must not be imagined as stupid drudges, for many of the slaves of the ancient world, sold to pay debts or captured in war, were both able and well-educated.

The analogy is appropriate because both the concepts of bond servitude and of stewardship are absolutely central to the Christian life. Christians, too, are not their own but "bought with a price" (1 Cor 6.19–20). Our lives are not ours to do with as we please but to invest in the service and will of another (Rom 12.1–2). It is not our mind but His mind which is important (Phil 2.5).

Christians are also stewards (1 Cor 4.1–2; 9.17; 1 Pet 4.10). All that they have, like themselves, belongs to another and must be diligently used to accomplish His purposes rather than their own (Luke 14.33).

Interestingly, the "talent" of this parable has no reference, as it now does, to abilities or skills. A talent in the world of Jesus stood usually for a large weight of silver money and was equivalent to about 6,000 drachma or denarii, one of which was the standard daily wage of a day laborer. But the impact of this parable was great enough to redefine the word. The idea of course lies in the Lord's statement that the lord of the servants distributed to them "each according to his own ability" (Matt 25.15). The "talents" simply came by association to stand for the God-given abilities which each person possesses and the responsibility which they bring with them.

So, according to the parable, the master of the servants took into consideration the varying abilities of his servants in determining what he left with them. None received a small sum. To one he gave five talents, to another two, and to a third, one. They were not all equally able, but they were all equally responsible, to faithfully invest what was given to them. This was a well-know business practice in the ancient world and from its very familiarity had the power to illustrate Jesus' point.

After a long time the master and owner returned from his journey abroad and called on his trusted servants for an accounting. The man who was given five talents and the man given two talents had both, by wise investment, doubled their money. Their story of faithfulness is essentially the same. But the focus of the parable is on the man who received one talent and promptly hid it in the ground. Was it an act of wisdom or folly? The master's response to his servants reveals the answer, and gives us valuable insight into the heart of the One who first told this story.

The Man Who Would Not Try (2)

> So he who had received five talents came and brought five other talents, saying, "Lord, you delivered to me five talents; look, I have gained five more talents besides them." His lord said to him, "Well done, good and faithful servant; you were faithful over a few things, I will make you ruler over many things. Enter into the joy of your lord." He also who had received two talents came and said, "Lord, you delivered to me two talents; look, I have gained two more talents besides them." His lord said to him, "Well done, good and faithful servant; you have been faithful over a few things, I will make you ruler over many things. Enter into the joy of your lord." (Matt 25.20–23)

The returning master judged the first two servants to be equally faithful, not by their gross gain, but by what they did with what they were given and the urgency with which both went to their tasks (immediately, 25.16 NASB). His praise for them is strong with emotion ("Well done!") and praise ("good and faithful servants").

Jesus' expectations of His followers is also tempered by their varying abilities (2 Cor 8.12) as He looks beyond the work to the man it reveals within. It is that wholeness of heart of which all men are capable that the Lord seeks (Deut 6.5; Mark 12.28–30). So He saw in a poor widow's mite a greater gift than the rich surplus of the wealthy (Mark 12.41–44). Love is its own taskmaster.

The body of Christ is enriched and empowered, not by a few super-heroes, but by each member serving humbly and earnestly "according to the grace that is given" to him (Rom 12.3–6); each one, like Mary, doing what he can (Mark 14.8). In this way the spiritual body grows and edifies itself in love (Eph 4.16). Real Christians seek service, not celebrity, and the glory is given to God (1 Cor 3.6).

But the focus of the parable is not on the two servants who

succeeded, but on the one who failed—the one-talent man. "Then he who had received the one talent came and said, 'Lord, I knew you to be a hard man, reaping where you have not sown, and gathering where you have not scattered seed. And I was afraid, and went and hid your talent in the ground. Look, you have what is yours'" (Matt 25.24–25).

If the servant expected credit for keeping his talent safe, or imagined some advantage in slandering his owner, he was sorely disappointed. His master dismisses his "fear" explanation as a ruse (had he really believed the master so hard he would have been more, not less, diligent, 25.26–27) and attributes his failure to an ungodly indifference and laziness—"You wicked and lazy servant…" (25.26). And if he saw his own trust as inconsequential beside that of his fellows, what but pride could allow the greater gifts of others to make him "unprofitable" (useless)? The one-talent man's lack of trading skills did not prevent him from opening a savings account with the local bankers (25.27). There is always a way for a Christian to serve His Savior however small it may appear. Love will never be useless.

This severe judgment on one guilty merely of neglect, not vice, bothers us. Some have yet to believe that sins of omission (failure to do what Christ commands) should be considered "wicked." "Wickedness" is reserved for gross immorality. Jesus obviously sees it otherwise. What we have not done is plainly not sufficient to make us profitable in His kingdom.

Modern disciples are still heard trying to excuse their indifferent service of Christ by declaring His teachings so demanding as to make obedience futile. It is a joke. People who say such things are slandering the gracious love of God in order to cover their own disinterest. It is the dismissal of such mercy that makes the severe judgment of those who will not even try entirely just (Heb 10.26–29). "And cast the unprofitable servant into the outer darkness. There shall be weeping and gnashing of teeth" (Matt 25.30).

As to the "joy of your lord," which the faithful servants were invited to share, what greater joy could there be for any child of God than to have the Lord of the universe look on him with approving delight and say, "Well done! good and faithful servant." Wouldn't we work a thousand life times for that! And then to think that He will consequently bring us to His side to serve Him in enterprises so unimaginably great that only eternity's vistas can reveal them—"...you were faithful over a few things, I will make you ruler over many" (Matt 25.21) "...and His servants shall serve Him" (Rev 22.3). It is that heart-thrilling anticipation that keeps the disciples of Jesus working in patient faithfulness until they see Him again.

The Final Crisis of the Parables

> When the Son of Man comes in His glory, and all the holy angels with Him, then He will sit on the throne of His glory. All the nations will be gathered before Him, and He will separate them one from another, as a shepherd divides his sheep from the goats. And He will set the sheep on His right hand, but the goats on the left. (Matt 25.31–33)

Gathered with His disciples at the end of that grueling Tuesday before His death, Jesus concludes a year of teaching by parables with a compelling vision of universal judgment (Matt 25.31–46). Jesus' stories had all along been pointing to a conclusion, a final time of accounting which would be pregnant for all with either tragedy or joy.

Several commentators speak of this saying of Jesus as the parable of the sheep and the goats though it is not a parable in the conventional sense. It is more a poetic description of the prophecy Jesus had spoken earlier that year at Caesarea Philippi (Matt 16.27). However rich with analogy, His language He is speaking of a real event.

But what does it mean? It is surrounded by controversy. Is Jesus speaking of a universal judgment of Christians only? of non-Christians only? or both? Are we to understand as social gospelers delightedly conclude that the sole basis of eternal judgment is how you treat the poor and distressed? Does faith in God and the Son not count? Does immorality not count? Is false doctrine of no concern? A careful look at what is said here along with all Jesus and the apostles have taught should answer these questions.

It was characteristic of Palestinian shepherds to pasture sheep with goats and at needful times to separate them. The metaphor of shepherd and sheep for God and His people was often used in the Old Testament (Psa 23; 100.3; Isa 40.11; Ezek 34.11–15) and is used by Jesus to describe His own relation to His disciples (John 10). In His illustration in Matthew 25, however, Jesus speaks of sheep and goats; and though the Lord seems to have specially focused His two preceding parables on the disciples there is no reason to believe that in these verses He has anything other in mind by "all the nations" than in Matthew 28.19 ("Go therefore and make disciples of all the nations") or Luke 24.47 ("and that repentance and remission of sins should be preached in His name to all nations..."). All nations are to be judged for the simple reason that the gospel has been preached to all.

And the basis of this great judgment? It seems to be wholly focused on each person's treatment of distressed and burdened people: To the "righteous" (sheep) on His right He says: "for I was hungry and you gave Me food; I was thirsty and you gave Me drink; I was a stranger and you took Me in; I was naked and you clothed Me; I was sick and you visited Me; I was in prison and you came to Me, and then to the cursed" (goats) on His left the very opposite (vv 34–43).

To interpret this unusual parable of judgment as exhaustive would be a very grave mistake. Such would suggest that Christ had no concern for our treatment of the rich and comfortable, or was indifferent to blasphemy, unbelief, and false teaching as well as drunkenness, sexual immorality and dishonesty, the very opposite being true (Matt 12.31; John 8.24; 14.6; Matt 7.15–16; 15.14; 16.11–12; 15.18–19; 19.9).

What the Lord is doing here is focusing in on selfishness and lack of compassion as a character trait that will cost its owner eternal life with a merciful and selfless Christ and put him in an eternal hell with a merciless and prideful devil. This illustration was never intended to be exhaustive. It was intended to emphasize the importance of practical righteousness as opposed to mere ecclesiastical piety. An ungodly professing, church-going person is still an ungodly person. A lack of mercy reflects no sense of mercy received and a heart that has never been crucified with Christ. (Of course it must also be said that a compassionate unbeliever is still lost in His faithless disobedience.)

In this very spirit, James warns those who take great pride in hearing God's word, never practicing it, professing great faith, but never living it (Jas 1–2). Faith, he says, is vital and expressive. When he illustrates what that means: "Pure and undefiled religion before God is this: to visit orphans and widows in their trouble, and to keep oneself unspotted from the world" (1.27) we need to realize that compassion is critical to acceptance with the Son of God; but we should not blunder into thinking that such is all there is to being a disciple of Jesus (Jas 2.10–12; 4.7–10).

The Teacher's parables are ended. There awaits now the time when He will come in judgment. Then it will be determined whether or not we have understood Him.

Also by Paul Earnhart

Invitation to a Spiritual Revolution
Studies in the Sermon on the Mount

Few preachers have studied the Sermon on the Mount as intensively or spoken on its contents so frequently and effectively as the author of this work. His excellent and very readable written analysis appeared first as a series of articles in Christianity Magazine. By popular demand it is here offered in one volume so that it can be more easily preserved, circulated, read, reread and made available to those who would not otherwise have access to it. Foreword by Sewell Hall. 173 pages, $9.99 (PB).

DEWARD
PUBLISHING COMPANY

Jesus and His Parables
Craig B. Manning

The parables of Jesus provide a wonderfully unique view of the kingdom of heaven. This is one of the very few books that, in addition to examining the words of Jesus, explore the first century world of Jesus to gain insight into the parables. His narratives telling of the kingdom were based on the historical, political, and cultural world of His day. This book bridges the 2,000 year gap between now and the time of Jesus to help understand the kingdom of heaven as revealed in the parables. 284 pages. $13.99 (PB)

Beneath the Cross: Essays and Reflections on the Lord's Supper
Jady Copeland and Nathan Ward (editors)

The Bible has much to say about the Lord's Supper. Almost every component of this memorial is rich with meaning—meaning supplied by Old Testament foreshadowing and New Testament teaching. The Lord's death itself is meaningful and significant in ways we rarely point out. In sixty-nine essays by forty different authors, *Beneath the Cross* explores the depths of symbolism and meaning to be found in the last hours of the Lord's life and offers a helpful look at the memorial feast that commemorates it. 329 pages. $14.99 (PB), $24.99 (HB)

Grace Does That?
Perry Hall

Can a topic be both overexposed yet underdeveloped? Perry Hall contends that this is the paradoxical nature of the subject of grace. With his unique style of writing, he investigates the grace that builds confidence, the grace that is sufficient, the grace that is understood, the grace that obligates, the grace that motivates, the grace that rekindles, and the grace that worships. 188 pages. $11.99 (PB)

Hello, I'm Your Bible
Jason Hardin

A practical guide to understanding and applying God's word of truth. Whether you've just been introduced to the Bible, you'd like to get reacquainted with the Scriptures, or you're looking to grow in your ability to help others in their walk of faith, *Hello, I'm Your Bible* can guide you into a deeper relationship with the God behind the living and active word. 156 pages. $9.99 (PB)

Soul Food: Lessons from Hearth to Heart
Dene Ward

Cooking has always been a part of Dene Ward's life. She grew up in a house where they were always feeding someone and followed that same path as a wife and mother. On the table, she has always offered a nourishing meal; she now offers this collection to feed your souls, lessons from her hearth to your heart. 148 pages. $9.99 (PB)

Things Most Surely Believed
Forrest D. Moyer

In these 16 brief sermons, Forrest Darrell Moyer has stated with beautiful clarity and simplicity, yet with compelling force, the Christian's "reason for hope" that is in him. He deals with the greatest themes the race has ever known—God, Christ, the cross, sin and redemption, the church, heaven and hell—yet he does it in language that the man in the pew, unskilled in the intricacies of theological vocabularies, can easily grasp. Foreword by Doy Moyer. New Introduction by Jefferson David Tant. 142 pages. $9.99 (PB)

For a full listing of DeWard Publishing Company books, visit our website:

www.deward.com

CPSIA information can be obtained
at www.ICGtesting.com
Printed in the USA
FFOW04n2221230615
14533FF